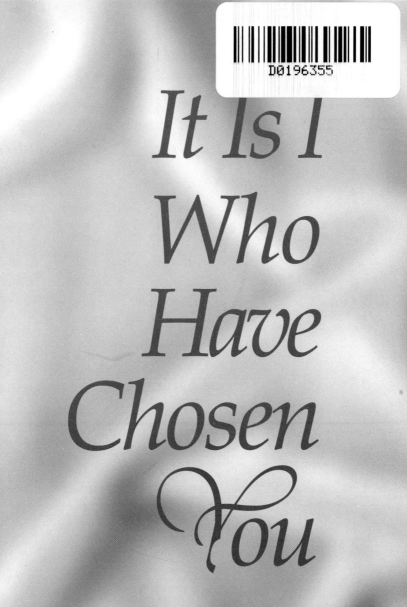

It Is I Who Have Chosen You

An Autobiography by
Judie Brown

American Life League
1997

Published by American Life League, Inc.
Printed by A.K.A. Printing and Mailing
Book design by Amy C. Jacobson

ISBN 1-890712-00-0

Printed in the United States of America

Dedication

I have often heard it said that behind every good man is a good woman, or vice versa. In my case that is truer than anyone will ever know. This update of my autobiography is being prepared just prior to the 30th wedding anniversary of Paul and Judie Brown. Our trials have been many, our joys have been exceedingly happy, and our family continues to be the source of surprises, the occasional difficulty and so much more.

And so I dedicate this book to my husband, Paul, without whom I could never have done so much of what God has called me to do. Paul Brown is my hero, he is my conscience, he is the source of my sanity, he is my counselor, and yes, sometimes he is difficult and stubborn and so am I! But as the song goes, he is the wind beneath my wings.

I love you, dear!

Table of

Prologue   **7**

Chapter 1:   A Mother's Love: No Matter What!   **8**

Chapter 2:   A Father for All Seasons 1953–1957   **14**

Chapter 3:   Going to K-Mart 1958–1964   **20**

Chapter 4:   Romancing the Blarney Stone 1964–1967   **26**

Chapter 5:   New Baby, New Battle 1968–1970   **34**

Chapter 6:   Blessed Are the Poor 1970–1972   **42**

Chapter 7:   In the School of Adversity 1973–1974   **50**

Chapter 8:   Hello, Congressman! 1975–1976   **58**

Chapter 9:   Mrs. Brown Goes to Washington 1976–1979   **64**

Chapter 10:   A Telegram From Heaven 1979–1980   **72**

Chapter 11:   We Will Never Forget You 1980–1981   **78**

Chapter 12:   True Vocation 1982–1983   **86**

Contents

Chapter 13:   The Wilting of the White House 1983–1985   **94**

Chapter 14:   If I Should Die Before I Wake 1985   **100**

Chapter 15:   On the Field, in the Courts, at the Polls 1986–1988 **106**

Chapter 16:   Matters of Opinion 1989   **114**

Chapter 17:   Betrayal and Unity 1990   **122**

Chapter 18:   Verbal Fog 1991–1992   **128**

Chapter 19:   God Never Makes a Mistake 1992 AT HOME   **134**

Chapter 20:   Goodbye, Daddy! 1993   **142**

Chapter 21:   Religious Right?   **146**

Chapter 22:   Celebrate *The Gospel of Life* 1995   **152**

Chapter 23:   Infanticide and Unity 1996   **158**

Chapter 24:   The Future Is Ours   **164**

Afterword   **172**

Prologue

It is not in my nature to write about myself. I believe sincerely that I am nothing more than God's servant and that I could accomplish nothing apart from His grace.

Yet I am also aware that each of us, as children of God, has a special mission in life, and that most of us periodically need to be refreshed in our awareness of that awesome truth. So I offer this account of my pilgrimage to date, in the hope that you may see—even in a life as ordinary as my own—that there is no aspect of life that is without purpose in God's plan. If we will allow the Lord to work through us, tremendous things can happen. Each day is a promise from God that life, while we have it, need never be wasted.

Walk with me then, through the past 52 years. Laugh with me, cry with me, celebrate with me, and mourn with me. See, if you will, the mystery of faith that continues to propel me even now: often beyond my understanding, sometimes even against my will, but always with the trust that in God everything has a purpose.

I am not suggesting that my life is a road map or model for others to follow. It surely is not. It is, however, a simple story of a simple woman who has come to know the value of faith and who has seen the Lord work because of it.

In the Gospel of John we learn of our union with Christ and how it comes about. We learn too that if we are open to the Lord's will in our lives, we soon understand how it is that He has chosen each one of us to be a part of His plan for all mankind.

Jesus says:

You are my friends if you do the things I command you. No longer do I call you servants, because the servant does not know what his master does. But I have called you friends, because all things that I have heard from my Father I have made known to you. You have not chosen me, it is I who have chosen you (John 15:14–16a).

Chapter

A Mother's Love: No Matter What!
1944–1952

As my mother never tired of pointing out, I entered the world a difficult and obstinate person. I was a "breech" baby, meaning that I tried to come out of the birth canal backwards. The doctors had to turn me around before I could be born. Even while I was still in the womb, I was giving others a challenge! Some things, my mother would say, never change.

This was in March 1944. My mother had been married to my father for a little longer than a year. My sister Sheila was born only 18 months later. Though I was too young to remember it, it was then that my life changed radically.

My father deserted us.

While my mother was still in Our Lady of Angels Hospital in Los Angeles recovering from Sheila's birth, my father had other fish to fry with a woman who took up the time that should have gone to his wife and family. Within a week of Sheila's birth, he was gone from our lives forever.

As it turned out, my mother had been his fifth wife—a fact she never knew.

The pain was intense at the time my father left. Mama's

One

In him who is the source of my strength, I have strength for everything.
Phil. 4:13

selfless love had been betrayed. Now she was left with two small babies and nowhere to go.

In later years my grandmother—Mama's mother, Bertha Tekla Baldi—told me how worried she was about my mother during this time. For months after the divorce Mama wept in anguish. She never let my sister or me see that side of her, though—she suffered in private. It was almost a year before she was able to start putting her life, and ours, back together again.

Ultimately we moved in with Grandma and Grandpa Baldi. They opened their hearts, and their modest home on Harcourt Avenue in Los Angeles, to the three of us. They made life as joyful for Mama as they could, always realizing that her dreams of home and family might be dashed forever.

How well I remember those years! Mama would leave for work each morning, leaving Sheila and me under the care of our doting grandparents. Grandpa worked as a bricklayer—when there was work to be found. When there wasn't, he stayed home and helped look after us. He played with us and talked with us, smoking his cigar and blowing big smoke rings in the air. He was cheerful and playful—until we did something to make Grandma upset. Then he got more than a little irritated with us.

This often happened when Grandma braided our hair. We would scream, yell at her, and call her names. She would become exasperated, bop us on the head with the brush, and call Grandpa in for reinforcement. We would end up in chairs in opposite corners of the dining room. But we never learned. The next time Grandma tried to braid our hair, we would raise Cain all over again.

Grandma and Grandpa, like all good Germans, believed in orderliness and obedience. The rules they set for us, and the standards of behavior to which they held us, were unbending. That doesn't mean that Sheila and I were especially orderly or obedient, however. We knew there would be consequences when we crossed the line. But we never let that stop us from crossing it anyway.

For example, Grandpa did not want us to take food to our room. But Sheila and I had other ideas and became very adept at crawling under the bed covers with cookies, milk, candy, chips, and other goodies we had smuggled out of the kitchen. Of course there was always incriminating evidence later on—crumbs, spills, and wrappers that we had left behind. But even being caught and punished didn't seem to spoil our desire to simply do it again the next night.

Right:
Bertha Tekla Shreck, my maternal grandmother, at her wedding to Louis W. Baldi; Harry and Elsie are behind them

Middle:
Grandma Baldi in 1951.

Far Right:
My mother upon her engagement to Chester Limbourne in 1952.

One of our favorite activities was helping Grandma with the laundry. She had one of those old-fashioned washing machines with a wringer. One day Sheila and I decided we could somehow speed up the process by sticking our hands into the tub and helping move the clothes around. You guessed it—I got my arm caught in the wringer. I screamed, Sheila screamed, and Grandma had a fit. After she freed my arm, I had the nerve to blame her for what had happened.

Not all my childhood experiences had to do with being naughty, though. I especially remember Wednesday nights, when I would go with Grandma to the weekly Rosary. We'd leave the house right after dinner and walk around the corner to the home of a neighbor lady. In her living room was a vigil candle and a beautiful statue of Our Lady crushing the head of the serpent. I remember kneeling next to Grandma on the hard floor—how it must have pained her aging knees—and being perfectly content to pray the entire Rosary. As we walked home I would ask why we couldn't go more often. I remember the smile on my mother's face when we got home. She could see that praying with Grandma was something I really loved to do.

Grandma and Grandpa loved us and were only too happy to do things to please us. Sheila and I quickly learned to exploit their

generous natures. Whenever the ice cream man came down our street, we could always rely on one or the other (or both) of them to treat us to a Popsicle. Sometimes we were able to orchestrate three or four treats in a single day! Needless to say, we both developed weight problems at an early age.

By the time I entered first grade at St. John's school, I was accomplished at manipulating others to get what I wanted. If I wanted to go home early, I told the teacher I was sick. If I wanted attention, I claimed to be having an asthma attack. If I complained loud enough and long enough, I always got my way. Except for the asthma attacks—some of which were quite real—Sheila could play all the same cards.

I shudder to think what sort of children we would have become had it not been for the man who entered Mama's life at about this time.

Chapter

A Father for All Seasons

1953–1957

Mama was still young, and quite attractive, and she had two younger brothers who were not unaware of those facts. It seemed they were always bringing someone home to meet her. I remember some of those fellows, and—to be quite frank—I'm thankful Mama had the good taste to pass on them.

All but one, that is.

Chester Limbourne came to know my mother through Uncle George, Mama's baby brother. I remember the first time Chester came to the house. I remember him coming many other times, to take Mama out for the evening. And I especially remember the night Mama talked to Grandma about getting married again—or, at first, about not getting married again.

Needless to say, our mother's marital status was a topic of great interest to Sheila and me, so we had our ears pressed to the door as Mama explained to Grandma why she felt she could not accept Chester Limbourne's proposal of marriage—even though she thought him the most wonderful man in the world.

Mama was 34 at the time, and she suffered from rheumatoid arthritis in her legs and arms. She had to go to downtown Los

Two

Husbands should love their wives as they do their own bodies. He who loves his wife loves himself. Observe that no one ever hates his own flesh; no, he nourishes it and takes care of it as Christ cares for the church—for we are members of his body.

Eph. 5:28–29

Angeles for "gold treatments" at City of Hope Hospital on a regular basis. She was afraid that her arthritis, combined with the fact that she had two children, would simply be too much for Chester for handle.

Sheila and I were horrified. We didn't know much about the world at that age, but we knew that we thought Chester Limbourne was terrific. He always gave us a big hug when he came for Mama, and he was so nice to Grandma and Grandpa. We were happy to see Mama with someone who was so nice, and we couldn't believe she'd pass up an opportunity to marry him.

Chester finally passed over all Mama's objections by focusing on the one thing that made marriage the right decision for her: He simply loved her more than anything else in the world, and he wanted more than anything to be her husband and our father.

From the moment they walked down the aisle, Sheila and I knew that we had a real father, someone who loved our mother and us, someone who cared about the security of our little family. Though we were not bone of his bone and flesh of his flesh, he always treated us as though we were. The sacrifices he made for us would require another book to recount.

And so, in 1951, we moved into a house of our own. Sheila and I had never seen Mama so happy. We almost didn't know what to make of it! But we never questioned that life was wonderful.

∽

Our little family was soon blessed by two additions. A brother, Mark, was born in 1952. Two years later my sister Ann arrived. The babies were the center of attention. I loved taking care of them for my mother, who was still bothered by her arthritis.

Mark required special care, because he was a special baby: He was born with Down syndrome. He seldom cried; in fact it seemed as though he always had a smile on his face, and whenever he became ill, Mama became very anxious—and with good reason.

Mark's immune system was underdeveloped, which meant that even the slightest sniffle could swiftly develop into a form of pneumonia. Every one of us did our best to protect him from germs, but from time to time he would catch cold and have to be nursed around the clock. When that happened, Mama, Sheila, and I had to team up. Mama would handle the night shift, and Sheila and I would take turns staying home from school so we could care for Mark during the day, while Mama slept.

In the fall of 1954, when he was two and a half years old, Mark came down with one of his occasional colds. But this time was different. He fell more gravely ill than he ever had before. He didn't respond to being touched. He was in a state of sleepiness from which he never seemed to completely awaken.

I came home from school one afternoon to find Mama in a panic. She was on the phone with the doctor. Before I knew it we were out the door, in the car, racing to the hospital. I sat next to Mama in the front seat, holding Mark in my lap. He was so weak he was barely breathing. It was a 15-minute ride to the hospital. Mark didn't make it. He died in my arms.

I'll never forget that awful afternoon. Daddy met us at the hospital. So did the doctor, who coldly pronounced Mark dead and then had the gall to tell us that we were all probably "better off."

Looking back, I'm sure my mother always knew that Mark's condition was such that he could not survive to adulthood.

But her faith enabled her to use each moment she spent caring for him as a testimony to her confidence that God would look after her son. She and Daddy always treated Mark and Ann as though they were equal, even though Mark was never able to walk or even to crawl. We used to sit together on Sunday evenings and watch the Walt Disney program. We all enjoyed it, but Mark enjoyed it more than anyone. Just hearing the theme song made him giggle and bounce up and down. Indeed, all music affected him that way—it made him happy.

We went through the next few days after Mark's death as if in a trance. Friends and family members flocked to our aid at once. Though each one offered loving sympathy, the loss was simply too much for my mother to bear. Against all reason, she blamed herself for what had happened. Wanting to be alone in her grief, she shut out everyone except Daddy—who was, as always, her rock, her fortress, her friend.

⚬⚬

Things only got tougher for Mama as the year went on. Her arthritis hit her harder than ever. She developed bleeding ulcers. She was hospitalized a couple of times. With each setback, Daddy grew stronger, more compassionate, more in love with this woman who was suffering so.

He also grew more demanding of the rest of us, to be patient with Mama, to love her, to avoid doing things that would upset her. Of course, all children hear their fathers scold them, "Don't upset your mother!" But I always felt that Daddy spoke more from a genuine concern for her well-being than from a simple desire to keep us in line. He loved her so much that he suffered with her, though he never suggested that her difficulties were weighing him down.

I still remember the small but beautifully decorated Christmas tree we placed at Mark's grave the year he died. I also remember Mama's tears as we placed the tree by his grave marker. It became an annual trip for us, and each time we felt the loss as keenly as though Mark had just left us the day before.

I see now that the aftermath of Mark's death was so severe precisely because of the unselfish love my parents had for him while he was alive. Had they cared less about him while he was alive, they would have cared less about his death. But from the moment he was born, when they rejected the doctor's suggestion that they put Mark in a home somewhere because he could never lead a "normal" life, my parents loved Mark as deeply as they loved all the rest of us.

Maybe it is fair to say they loved him even more, because his needs were so much greater. He required long, hard hours of care, which they surely would rather have spent doing something else; but they never stinted. He needed to be at home virtually all the time, which many would find inconvenient; but they never complained. There was simply nothing they would not have done for their son, while at the same time making sure that my sisters and I never felt left out.

Looking back on this hectic period, I cannot help but wonder how Daddy coped with the powerful emotions that must have welled up inside him. Mama's rapid deterioration meant he never really had time to mourn the death of his only son. I wonder how many other men would have handled it the way he did, always placing his wife's needs first? I was too young to appreciate what he was going through, or the grace with which he handled it.

I know only that no words can do justice to his role in our family through those dark days. Is it any wonder that I consider Chester Limbourne such a great man?

Chapter

Going to K-Mart
1958–1964

Gradually life began to level out. Ann, the baby of the family, turned three. I turned 13—a very large 13, I might add. I was seriously overweight. Had I been a boy, I'm sure I could have been a star lineman on the high school football team.

Mama's arthritis seemed to recede a bit. She moved a bit slower than she would have liked, but she managed to do pretty much everything she wanted to do. And she had a lot of things she wanted to do. She served as chauffeur for the nuns at our local grade school and as head chef for the big weekly dinners we held at our house for all the family—as many as 20 people each week. She prepared baked goods for the church whenever they asked, made most of our clothes, and even held down a part-time job stuffing envelopes and collating materials for a local business. She never complained, never made excuses, never asked for sympathy. She just did what she felt she should do and made the best of her physical limitations.

Somehow, in spite of all this, she still had the ability to be there for us when we needed her. She simply seemed to radiate love to others. Neither Ann, Sheila, nor I ever brought home a "stranger."

Three

I will instruct you and show you the way you should walk; I will counsel you, keeping my eye on you.

Psalm 32:8

Everyone was welcome; everyone was made to feel part of the family. In fact, countless numbers of our friends came home with us after school, or dropped in on weekends, just to talk with Mrs. Limbourne, the wonderful lady who always had time to listen, a good word to say, and a warm smile with brown eyes that could cut right through your troubles.

We were just an ordinary family, dealing with the problems that everyone faced in the late 1950s. There was a budget that allowed for only short vacations, three young girls who never seemed to stop arguing—all the normal things you might remember (or choose to forget) about your own childhood.

When I turned 16, Daddy decided to take on the job of teaching me to drive. We went to the Hollywood Race Track, in suburban Inglewood, which had a huge parking lot. Daddy figured I'd need plenty of room if I were to avoid endangering the safety of others. And he was right. To this day I cannot parallel park. I even have trouble backing up. I'm not the person you'd want to have at the wheel in a tight situation.

It was also about this time that I decided to begin a chapter of the Johnny Mathis Fan Club. I answered an ad in a teen magazine from someone in Maine who was looking for help expanding the club. I wrote tons of letters and made hundreds of long-distance phone calls. I finally found myself president of the largest chapter of the entire fan club. I wrote regularly to Johnny Mathis, of course, whom I adored but had never met. I recounted all the details of how the fan club was growing, trusting that he pored over every word I wrote.

Then, one day, the phone rang. It was Johnny Mathis's agent. Johnny was going to be making an appearance soon at the Coconut Grove and wanted to invite my parents and me to come as his personal guests. After the show, we were invited backstage to meet Johnny in his dressing room. I was in heaven!

Looking back, I marvel at my parents' patience through all this. They never told me I was being a silly teenage girl, never even complained about the cost of all those letters and phone calls. They just supported me in what I wanted to do, believing that children were better served if they had wholesome activities that helped them understand the ways of the world.

They sacrificed for us in so many ways—music lessons twice a week for 10 years, new clothes when we simply "had to have them," an excellent (and expensive) education at the parish school. When I think of the many things they must have had to do without, I'm saddened by the fact that as a child I never appreciated, let alone thanked them for, all that they did for me. If anything, I only grew more demanding, and more outspoken when I didn't get my way. It took me a long time to learn what Daddy so often told me, "Money doesn't grow on trees, Judie!"

Right:
Me,
two years.

Center: Me,
age six,
first grade.

Far right:
Me in
Mexico,
1953.

But I began to learn the value of a dollar when I started taking various part-time jobs. I delivered Fuller Brush products for a local salesman. I taught beginning accordion at the studio where I myself took lessons. I filled in behind the jewelry counter of the nearby Kresge's five-and-dime. None of these jobs demanded a great deal of time, but they did begin to teach me the importance of commitment and hard work.

I also volunteered as a "candy striper," or nurse's aide, at the local hospital. I was easily bored, and needed lots of activities to keep me busy. Working in the hospital didn't bring in any money, but it taught me some important lessons. It cemented a lesson I had learned from the way we had cared for Mark: Those who are suffering are the ones for whom we must make time. I still remember the faces of patients who would see me and know that I would always stop and talk with them for a while, even if they were not going to buy one of my candy bars or packages of Kleenex. My grandfather lived right across the street from the hospital—he had moved there after Grandma died—and I would visit him, too, cleaning up the apartment or just chatting.

∞

As high school graduation approached, the time came to settle on some more stable plans for the future. I knew I wanted to go to college, and at first I thought I wanted to be a child psychologist. I had good grades and was accepted at every college to which I applied. I was even offered a full scholarship to New York University. But I turned it down because I realized my career goals were not sufficiently well planned to leave my family and go 3,000 miles away. My parents were thrilled by the honor of my being offered the scholarship—and relieved, I think, when I decided not to accept it.

I weighed all my options and discussed things at length with my parents. We talked a lot about the medical profession, with which I was so enamored. Mama was afraid that my inclination to become personally involved with anyone who had a problem might be my undoing. I had to agree.

We finally determined that the business world provided the best fit for my talents. So I stayed at home, stayed on at the local

Kresge's—I had by now become bookkeeper for the entire store—and registered for the fall semester at a local college.

A year later I decided it was time to move out and live on my own. I took an apartment just a few blocks from my parents' house. Not long after, my father finalized a decision he had been contemplating for some time: The family would move away. My baby sister, Ann, was now eight years old, and Daddy wanted her to have a horse and a big yard and the kind of environment that southern California could no longer provide. And so, in the summer of 1963, Mama and Daddy and Sheila and Ann packed up and moved to Oregon, while I remained in Los Angeles.

My career was developing nicely. Within a few months I had been promoted from the local store to the western regional headquarters of what was now known as the K-Mart Corporation. I continued my studies, worked under a couple of brilliant corporate vice presidents, and within a year was invited to become the western regional office manager—a position that had never before been offered to a woman of only 21.

After consulting my family, I accepted the promotion. It meant a lot of travel, and discontinuing my education, but it seemed like the right step. I began criss-crossing the 11 states in K-Mart's western region, overseeing training for new stores and meeting people who were in upper-level management positions with the company.

One of these was a very interesting man named Paul Brown.

Chapter

Romancing the Blarney Stone

1964–1967

Traveling around the western United States in the early 1960s was a great job for a young woman. I had freedom, I had a good salary, and I had the responsibilities of an executive and the perks that went with them.

Frankly, it has always been a bit hard for me to understand why some women complain about the difficulties of competing in the job world. I can honestly say I never faced any sort of discrimination. I worked hard, I did my job well, and I was recognized and rewarded for it. What has changed since those days? Has the business world suddenly turned against talent and hard work? Or have women begun trying to imitate or replace men, rather than complement and support them? In any case, my own corporate adventure was wonderful.

One of my first assignments, in the fall of 1964, was to help open a new store in Ogden, Utah. This particular store had special importance to the company: It was going to pioneer a new design. An experienced manager, a Mr. Paul A. Brown, had been assigned to oversee the opening and to make sure that the layout of the store was perfect, right down to the last tube of toothpaste.

Four

Love never fails. There are in the end three things that last: faith, hope and love, and the greatest of these is love.

1 Cor. 13:13

Mr. Brown, I was told, was bright, energetic, and experienced. There was just one problem: For some reason, he absolutely refused to punch in and out on his time card, yet he insisted on being paid overtime. Since part of my job was to serve as supervisor of payroll, one of my first tasks was to set Mr. Brown straight.

I went looking for him one Thursday afternoon as my staff was trying to complete the week's payroll. I found him squatting down in front of a display case, arranging merchandise on the bottom shelf.

"Mr. Brown?" I asked.

He didn't even look up. "Yeah," he muttered.

"Mr. Paul A. Brown?" I asked, using my most intimidating supervisory tone of voice.

Now he looked up. "What do you want?" he snapped.

"It's about your overtime," I said. "You haven't been punching in your time card, and I can't pay you until you do."

"Go to h___."

Well! I stood over him, all 210 pounds of me, and gave him a stern lecture on K-Mart company policy. The company would not allow me to pay his overtime, I said, if he did not record the hours. The company was most generous with managers like himself, I said, but the company also needed a record, so . . .

He didn't say anything. He just stood up, glared at me for a second, then shook his head and walked away. As far as I know, he never did punch a time card—he probably felt it was too demeaning for a manager—and he never got paid for his overtime.

I, of course, was speechless with anger. Nobody was going to talk to Judie Limbourne like that! For the next three years, whenever our paths crossed, I always found some way to insert a snide remark or otherwise express my dislike for him.

So you can imagine my reaction when a friend suggested, some three years later, that I call a halt to the feud. It was embarrassing to the company, she said, and it couldn't possibly be doing my career any good. Besides, she said, Paul Brown was really a

Paul and I dating, 1967.

Bottom right: My engagement photo.

warm, friendly person, and she was sure I'd like him if I would only give him a chance.

Well, I thought why not? It had been three years, after all. A lot of water had flowed under the bridge. I had advanced in position and salary. I had lost 80 pounds. I was driving a Lincoln Continental, which I thought was pretty good for a 23-year-old woman. And the store he now managed was only an hour's drive away, in Bellevue, Washington. So, one Wednesday afternoon, I drove the 50 miles to Bellevue and dropped in on my old nemesis.

Mr. Brown was extraordinarily polite. We chatted about the "business" I had come to discuss, then he walked me to my car. Before I drove off, he asked if he could call me. I said yes.

That was how our relationship started. In the coming weeks we had several dates, a number of long conversations, and more than a few stormy disagreements.

Right: Walking down the aisle with Daddy.

Below: The wedding party, December 30, 1967.

One date was especially memorable. We went out to dinner with a couple whom Paul had known since childhood. The man had retired from the military and had invited us to be his guests at the officers' club at Sandy Point naval base on Puget Sound. It was lovely and romantic. Music flowed from a juke box in the corner, and Paul and I danced for hours. Finally, while Frank Sinatra sang "Strangers in the Night," Paul asked me marry him.

I did what any love-struck 23-year-old would have done under the circumstances—I laughed at him.

I hadn't known him all that long, but I knew him well enough to know that he had a full complement of Irish mischief in his personality. The proposal, I was sure, was just part and parcel of the Paul A. Brown mystique—another bit of blarney. So I laughed.

But when Paul asked me again, and I could see in his eyes that he was sincere, I didn't laugh any more. I just looked back at him and said, "Yes."

Many people have been astounded by how brief our courtship was. I must admit, sometimes I myself have looked back on it in wonderment. But both Paul and I somehow knew from the start that we were like a hand in a glove, made for each other. I truly believe God had a hand in this from the beginning. In any case, over the next few weeks we had several serious conversations, which convinced me beyond a doubt that there was no one else in the entire world with whom I would rather spend the rest of my life. I knew I now had two of the most wonderful men in the world deeply involved in my life.

I couldn't wait to tell my mother. She was my confidante, the only person I trusted with my deepest feelings, my fears, my dreams, the cares of my heart and soul. She was always a good listener and a wise counselor, a beacon of light in the darkness. Whenever I had something important to talk about, I always relied on her guidance and advice.

So when I called to tell her that Paul and I were engaged and planning to be married that December, I was eager to hear her response.

"Judie," she said at once, "this will never last. You haven't known him long enough."

As we talked, I understood her reservations more clearly.

She had only met Paul once before, wh_ for a weekend, and had been less than imp_ Paul had been quiet around the family, almos_ he was nervous, meeting the people he was plan_ in-laws. Perhaps he was just put off by the (admittea_ _se of humor that prevailed in our home. In any case, he h_ _ been himself, and my mother had come away convinced that he was not the man for me.

Even so, Mama respected my ability to make decisions for myself, and she was happy to see me so happy. In the end, she gave us her blessing.

The engagement was brief and occasionally stormy. My parents had the wedding announcements printed and in the mail when Paul and I had a huge argument one night and called off the whole thing. When I told Mama, she took it in stride. The cancellation notices, she assured me, could be in the mail within 72 hours. Fortunately it took Paul and me only 48 hours to make up, and the wedding was on again. Everything moved along peacefully from that point onward.

∽

Barely three months after that magical evening at the naval base, Paul and I were married at the same church in Hawthorne, California, where I had received my first Holy Communion as a little girl. The wedding had been planned long distance. My parents had moved back to California a few years before, and my mother's health had begun to deteriorate again, so I handled as many of the details as I could from Washington, where I was working.

I remember every detail of that day, much as I am sure you remember your own wedding day. The flowers were perfect, the church was magnificent, the priest was magnanimous, and magic filled the air. I remember wishing that my grandparents could have been there, as I knew they would have been pleased. I wished that my mother could have been completely healthy.

But most of all I remember my parents and the joy they exuded. Paul, who was proving to be one of the most complex and intriguing people I had ever known, had by now managed to endear himself to my family, and they couldn't have been happier for us.

people had given so much and sacrificed so selflessly, only for me but also for my sisters. Now they watched me begin a new family which I would always hope to model after the lessons I had learned in my own childhood. Their tears of joy were part of what made that day so perfect.

After a honeymoon in San Francisco, Paul and I set up housekeeping in a brand-new apartment in Seattle. A whole new phase of life was beginning for this obstinate woman of German descent and this marvelous man who reflected every characteristic for which the Irish are famous, from his grand sense of humor to his total dedication to family.

Chapter

New Baby, New Battle

1968–1970

My first official action as Mrs. Paul A. Brown was to resign my position with K-Mart. The job still required a lot of travel, and Paul and I felt that wouldn't be good for our marriage. Paul himself had left the company a month before our wedding, because the prospect of relocating every six to eight months—not uncommon for those on the management track—seemed too disruptive. Besides, we had both grown attached to the Seattle area.

I took a job with the now-defunct White Front stores, a chain of discount retail outlets similar to K-Mart. I was head bookkeeper for their store in Tacoma. Paul entered management training with White Front, overseeing a store in Seattle. The two stores were 13 miles apart. We bought a small home about halfway between them, adopted a Weimaraner puppy, and began settling into married life.

But not into family life, precisely. We had decided to wait a while before having children. I went to a gynecologist to get a prescription for birth control pills. At this time, neither Paul nor I had any qualms about the pill; neither of us had been exposed to anything that would suggest that there was anything wrong, either

Five

The Lord keeps faith; he it is who will strengthen you and guard you against the evil one.

2 Thess. 3:3

medically or morally, with using it. For us, it was a simple proposition: We didn't want to start a family just yet, and taking the pill was the most effective way to prevent pregnancy.

There was only one problem.

After examining me, the gynecologist told me that it was a little late to be investigating birth control—I was already six weeks pregnant!

After the initial shock wore off, Paul and I were ecstatic. We picked out colors for the baby's room, began setting aside as much money as we could, and shared the good news with anyone who had a telephone. On November 23, 1968, after 12 hours of difficult labor, Hugh Richard Brown III was born. We named him after Paul's father, who had died before Paul and I met. Naturally, Hugh was the most beautiful baby anyone had ever had.

We did all the usual things that new parents do. We bought a crib and toys and a bassinet, we read every book we could get our hands on about what to do when the baby cried, we made faces about the dirty diapers and fumbled with the diaper pins. We did everything except have the baby baptized.

Let me explain. I had been a lukewarm Catholic, at best. Paul, though he had been raised a Catholic, had long since lost interest in it and for the first two years of our marriage refused to have anything to do with it.

I was a willing accomplice, to be sure, in our decision to ignore Sunday Mass. Paul and I would tell ourselves that Sunday was our only real time to be with the baby, so it made sense to skip church, stay home, and enjoy our little family. I occasionally put up token resistance, and I think Paul and I both knew our thinking was quite selfish. But in the end, when Sunday morning rolled around, we stayed home.

When Hugh was born, the subject of baptism came up briefly, but Paul vehemently refused even to consider it. He wouldn't have his child baptized into a faith he himself was not practicing. And that was that.

At the same time, because Hugh's birth had been so difficult on me, the doctor recommended that I use the pill in order to avoid becoming pregnant again right away. My body was in a severely weakened state, he said, and another pregnancy following so soon after the first might have serious consequences. I needed time to recover, he said—at least two years.

Me, Hugh, age one month, & Baron von Schnell Blitz Brown.

Far right: Hugh, at three months..

By now I had read enough about the pill to have serious misgivings about its health consequences, so I asked if I could use an IUD instead. My doctor, who was a practicing Catholic, approved my request and inserted the device without comment. He never told me that the IUD is, in effect, an abortifacient; he never suggested that I discuss the matter with a priest; he never said one word to me about the matter other than "okay."

This took place in January 1969. Hugh had been born two months before. *Humanae Vitae*, the Church's statement on birth control, had been issued eight months before. It is an indication of the state of my Catholicism that I had no idea the Church did not condone any artificial birth control, nor did anyone ever tell me this was the case. At that stage in my spiritual life, knowing the Church's position might not have mattered to me anyway. In any case, I got the IUD.

∽

While Hugh was still an infant, Paul left White Front and became an insurance salesman. He worked with several different companies before settling in with one of the country's largest and best-known organizations. Almost immediately he became their top salesman.

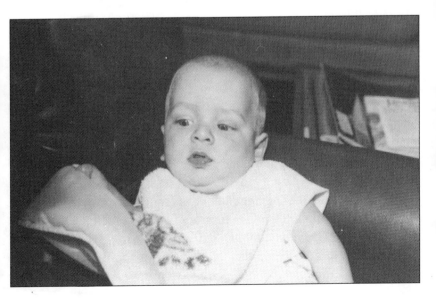

One weekend Paul was in San Francisco, attending a sales seminar, when he called me late one night. He sounded excited. "Judie," he said, "I want you to make an appointment with the priest at the local parish. I want to go to confession and return to the Church."

I had no idea where this new line of thinking had come from. Perhaps Paul had been rethinking our conversations about baptizing Hugh, or the foolish ways we justified skipping Mass on Sundays. Perhaps someone at the seminar said something that challenged Paul to renew his faith—which, I believe, had never really died but simply gone into "spiritual hibernation." I had no insight at all into the process. I only knew the result: We were going back to church.

Frankly, I was relieved. Despite all the reassurances we gave each other that what we were doing was okay, I knew in my heart that we had turned our backs on the Church—on the Lord—for no good reason other than laziness, and I could never shake the nagging thought that if anything were to happen to either of us, we were headed straight for hell.

I had thought on more than one occasion of simply bundling up the baby and going to Mass by myself, but I was afraid Paul would be angry. During those early months and years of marriage, while we were still struggling to adjust to each other, I guess I was insecure enough that I didn't want to provoke any disagreements that might turn into fights that might turn into separation and divorce. Silly, perhaps, but that was what I feared might happen. That, plus a heavy dose of my own lukewarmness, was more than enough to keep me away from church.

But Paul's phone call changed everything. I contacted the pastor, Fr. Willonberg, the very next morning. I explained to him that both Paul and I wanted to come back to church, wanted to make a general confession and receive the sacraments, and wanted to have our son baptized. He didn't bat an eye, God bless him.

Soon all the arrangements were made. We visited Fr. Willonberg and made our confessions. What a feeling of warmth and security! The next Sunday we went to Mass. Hugh, now 18 months old, was baptized that morning. Not too many babies are able to walk forward to be baptized, wearing a suit, and chatting with the priest all the while, but that's how it was for Hugh. We had called the couple who had hosted us for that fateful dinner at the Naval Officers' Club and asked them to be Hugh's godparents. All in all, it was quite a week.

It was also at about this time that I had the IUD removed—not because of any convictions about either its abortifacient properties or the Church's position on birth control; we were still ignorant on those topics. We had simply decided that we wanted to have more children and didn't want to wait. I had recovered sufficiently from Hugh's birth that the health risk was largely removed, and I had taken quite well to being a full-time wife and mother. Paul and I decided we wanted six children, and we couldn't wait to get started. By the next summer, Baby Brown number two was on the way.

∾

By this time we were attending Mass regularly. In fact, it was while we were at Mass one Sunday that Fr. Willonberg said something that would turn our lives upside down.

He spoke, with great distress, of a referendum question that was to be on the ballot in Washington state that November. The purpose of the referendum was to liberalize the state's abortion law.

Abortion. In those days the word still had the power to shock people, and it shocked Paul and me that Sunday morning. Here we were, brand-new parents with a baby on the way, newly returned to the faith of our childhood, hearing a sermon about people who wanted to kill little babies with the full consent of the law. It felt as though the earth had moved under our pew. How, I wondered, could a mother willfully seek the destruction of her own child?

I was soon to find out, however, that there were many women who thought nothing of it, who thought that their own sexual freedom should supersede any other claims, who thought they should have the right to do away with the "problems" created by their own choices and actions.

So when Fr. Willonberg invited us to work with him, distributing pro-life literature door to door and asking our neighbors and friends to be sure to vote "no" on Referendum 20, Paul and I were eager to get involved. That was the beginning of our battle to save little children like our own, whose lives had begun so simply but with such miraculous heavenly intervention.

∽

Today, years later, people often tell me how inane the arguments of the pro-death forces seem to them. I take no pleasure in telling them that in 1970, in Washington state, the arguments were exactly the same. Then, as now, there were people who believed that not all human beings were created equal and that the law should permit some human beings to murder other human beings when it suited their convenience. People were just as selfish and depraved then as they are now.

The only difference is that then there were no organized pro-life groups ready and willing to fight for the rights of the pre-born. Just five months after our rag-tag group began its door to door campaign, the people of the state of Washington said yes to abortion in a close vote.

We were crushed. How could it have happened? Where would it end? How could we stop it?

Chapter

Blessed Are the Poor
1970–1972

As it turned out, the 1970 referendum defeat in Washington state was far from the only blow our family was to suffer that year. They say that adversity is a great teacher. Well, the Lord chose 1970 to shower us with painful lessons.

That summer, amid the frenetic door to door literature campaign, we took a Sunday afternoon off and went to a company picnic. A lot of the dads were taking their kids down an especially high, steep slide on the playground. Paul took Hugh down the slide a couple of times, much to their mutual delight. For some reason, on the third time down they picked up more speed than before. Afraid that he might drop Hugh onto the concrete playground surface, Paul clutched him tightly with both arms and then tried to stop by digging his heels into the hard surface.

The result—a shattered kneecap, several weeks in and out of the hospital, a full leg cast for six months, inability to pursue his career as a salesman, and the sudden realization that although he was the number-one salesman for a major insurance company, he had never sold himself a disability policy!

Because he worked strictly on commission, this meant no

Six

I was hard pressed and was falling, but the Lord helped me. My strength and my courage is the Lord, and he has been my savior.

Psalm 118:13–14

income for our family. Here we were with one baby and another on the way, a mortgage, two car payments, a pile of credit card bills, and no way to pay them. What followed was humbling and anguishing—but, in God's master plan, much to our benefit.

I had some unemployment insurance coming to me, for which I applied. Paul received a small check as well. We quickly learned how to survive on $20 a week for groceries. When we fell hopelessly behind with our bills, we filed for bankruptcy and homesteaded our house, a legal maneuver that enabled us to stay in our home without bank foreclosure until we could regain a steady a income and pay down our debts.

In time, we did exactly that. But the intervening six months were just awful. I am still grateful to our neighbors, who really pitched in and helped us. They understood our predicament and they were there for us. Not once did they speak or act in a way that added to the embarrassment I knew Paul was feeling. And to think it all happened because he took his son down a playground slide one summer afternoon!

Our main form of entertainment was going to the drive-in movie once a week. It was cheap, and it enabled Paul to stretch out his leg in the back seat. Besides, we couldn't affore a baby-sitter, and going to the drive-in made it possible to take Hugh with us.

Paul started to go stir crazy more than once during that period. The combination of boredom, embarrassment, and frustration was almost more than he could handle. But he never lost his perspective. I was the one who did that! I would burst into tears over what I saw as the hopelessness of our situation. Having worked as a credit manager for so many different stores, the idea of declaring personal bankruptcy was especially galling to me. But Paul would firmly assure me that we would survive and that we would never experience such an ordeal again, as long as he had anything to say about it.

∽

Paul was still in the midst of his rehabilitation when the second little Brown made her appearance on the scene. And a memorable appearance it was! We were having Sunday brunch at a neighbor's house—I was tucking into a short stack of pancakes with peach preserves—when the first labor pangs hit. Remembering how long the labor process had been with Hugh, I wasn't overly concerned. I casually mentioned to Paul that after breakfast we should probably consider starting off for the hospital.

We very nearly didn't make it. Catherine Marie Brown (named for her two grandmothers) was born just three hours later. Paul was able to be present for the delivery and was the first one to hold her—the nurses cleaned her up and presented her to him with a tiny pink bow in her hair. He was one proud father. "Judie, I was really praying for a girl," he told me. "I'm the youngest of four boys, so I especially wanted a daughter."

Cathy's big brother was also quite enthusiastic upon her arrival home. He could hardly wait to hold her, feed her, give her a bath, and do anything else I was willing to let him try. Actually, life was quite a panic in the Brown household during those first few weeks. Between the new baby, little Hugh—who was only two and a half—and Paul, who was still hobbled by his knee injury, it was hard to keep track of just exactly who was taking care of whom. We even had neighbors dropping in to help Hugh help Paul take care of

Cathy so that I could take care of everything else. If you think it sounds confusing, you should have been there to see it!

Two months after Cathy was born I went back to the doctor, and to our pastor, to discuss birth control. The danger still existed with regard to my health. My womb had been seriously weakened during Cathy's delivery, and my body was too weak to withstand another pregnancy any time soon. So, with the blessing of a Catholic priest and a doctor who was also a Catholic, another IUD was inserted.

It astonishes me now, looking back on the experience, that both our priest and our doctor were either ignorant of what the Catholic Church teaches on birth control, or simply delinquent in their duty to tell young couples the truth. For my part, I had no idea I was doing anything that the Church taught was wrong. How was I to know, if the only people who could have told me, didn't? No one ever told me that IUDs were supposed to be painless, so when this one caused me discomfort I didn't think anything of it. Maybe it was the Lord's way of trying to penetrate my ignorance, to let me know something was amiss. If so, I missed the hint.

∽

The day finally came when Paul was able to walk again without assistance. He told me he wanted to return to K-Mart and resume his career there, if he could, though it would likely mean moving away from our home and our friends. I wasn't eager to pull up stakes and start over in a strange place, but we talked it over thoroughly and I finally told Paul that if going back to K-Mart was what he thought was right, then I was with him.

K-Mart welcomed him back with open arms (as I knew they would) and promptly offered him an attractive management position—in Atlanta, Georgia. What a shock! Here we were with two little children, a terrific job offer, and no money.

We borrowed from every relative who had a dollar to spare, bought a used 1957 Dodge that gave new meaning to the word "klunker," piled our two little babies and our large German Shepherd dog into the back, and hit the road. We decided to go by way of Los Angeles, so that my parents could see the babies and so that my master-mechanic stepfather could fix up the car that was going to have to carry us to what, as far we were concerned, might as well have been the other side of the earth.

Our two weeks in Los Angeles were marvelous. My parents were delighted to spend so much time with their grandchildren, even though my mother's arthritis had advanced to the point where she had great difficulty even holding a baby for any length of time. I had the sinking feeling that she would soon be completely unable to move. But we did all we could to make our visit special for her.

From Los Angeles we set off on our trek. We crossed the southern tier of the country, finally arriving in Savannah, Georgia, on the Atlantic coast. Paul's mother and oldest brother lived there, and the kids and I bunked with them while Paul went on to Atlanta to find a place for us to live. Three weeks later we moved into a small, dirty, run-down rental house, got our furniture and belongings out of storage, and settled in to our new life. It wasn't much, but it was home. The stressfulness of the whole experience was reflected in my body in a very visible way. I had lost 80 pounds during the latter part of my Washington days. Now I gained them back.

∽

Because we needed additional income, I took care of people's children during the day—and sometimes for a couple weeks at a time when their parents had to travel out of town on business. I was also able to volunteer some of my time on behalf of the local

Me, Paul, Cathy
at five months, and
two and a half-year-
old Hugh.

chapter of Birthright, which worked to provide housing for women who were pregnant and who might otherwise seek an abortion. I was able to collect items for Birthright baby showers while keeping the children in the car.

I soon came in contact with the leaders of Georgia Right to Life, a fledgling group just gearing up in early 1973. I assembled newsletters, stuffed them into envelopes, and dropped them off at the post office. The mailing list had only 200 names on it, but in those early days that seemed like a huge number.

Gradually things began to turn around for the Brown family. Paul's salary from K-Mart enabled us to get out of debt once and for all. It also enabled me to stop baby-sitting—a real blessing, as our own children needed more of my time. I lost the 80 pounds again.

I also increased my involvement with Birthright and with Georgia Right to Life. The Supreme Court had recently issued its infamous *Roe v. Wade* decision, which with a single stroke threw out the abortion laws of all 50 states, and for all practical purposes guaranteed abortion on demand at any point in the baby's prenatal development. Working for the pro-life cause now seemed to Paul and me to be a moral imperative.

Though Paul was working 70 to 80 hours a week, he always made time to keep abreast of what was happening in the movement. There was a lot of optimism in those days that the Supreme Court's reckless action would swiftly be overturned by an act of Congress. Paul thought that optimism was naive and foresaw a national tragedy of enormous proportions if abortion were indeed allowed to remain legal. I'm sad to say he turned out to be absolutely correct.

∾

Before long Paul was promoted again, this time to a senior management position. As always, a promotion meant a relocation. This time we were off to Kannapolis, North Carolina, where, among other things, we finally learned what the Catholic Church really taught about birth control.

I know it is difficult to understand how we remained ignorant of this teaching for so long. The truth, I suppose, is that we didn't really want to know the truth. We had been raised Catholic, and we understood the basics of the creed and the sacraments. We were going to Mass every Sunday and raising our children as good Catholics. In the early years of our marriage, when we sought out our pastor and a Catholic physician for advice on the subject of birth control, I suppose they simply told us what they thought we wanted to hear—that taking the pill, or using an IUD, was acceptable—second best, perhaps, but still okay.

Our lack of understanding isn't all that surprising, I suppose; I still run into many people who, despite being lifelong Catholics, don't understand anything more about the Church's teaching in this area than we did.

But when our pastor in Kannapolis finally shared with us the Church's full teaching about the sanctity of marriage, the full meaning of the procreative act, and the evil of birth control as a denial of trust in God, we didn't hesitate. The IUD came out, once and for all.

Thus our move to Kannapolis signaled the start of new era in an important part of our lives. As we were soon to learn, it signaled many other changes as well.

Chapter

In the School of Adversity

1973–1974

Talk about sending a lamb into the lion's den! We had barely unpacked the moving crates when I suddenly found myself engaged in a public debate with Kannapolis's leading proponent of abortion.

It started innocently enough. We had been getting acquainted with our parish priest, who was trying to raise the parish's awareness of abortion and who had decided that a public debate with the local abortionist would be a good idea. When he heard of my past involvement with Birthright and Georgia Right to Life, he decided I would be the perfect person to represent the pro-life side. And for some reason I'll never understand, I agreed to do it.

Remember, I had no training in debate, and no experience at it either. All I'd ever done as a pro-life volunteer was to stuff envelopes and transport items to garage sales. My opponent, Dr. Crosby (not his real name), was one of the most highly respected obstetrician/gynecologists in the area. He obviously wasn't too intimidated at the prospect of debating a pregnant (by this time our third little one was on the way) housewife from the rental district of Kannapolis. What would someone like me know about the

Seven

Dismiss all anxiety from your minds. Present your needs to God in every form of prayer and in petitions full of gratitude. Then God's own peace, which is beyond all understanding, will stand guard over your hearts and minds, in Christ Jesus.

Phil. 4:6–7

complex issues surrounding abortion?

Good question. The answer was that I knew hardly anything about the complex issues. So I stuck to the simple ones: When my turn came to speak, I simply described what actually happens to a baby during an abortion procedure. This so unnerved Dr. Crosby that he actually got up and walked out of the room!

Lesson number one in Kannapolis: God uses those who are willing to be used, and He gives them whatever they need to accomplish the task He sets before them.

∾

Life continued to be chaotic, even beyond the usual dislocations caused by moving. I had to go to work again, in order for us to send Hugh, who was now five, to a Christian kindergarten. I eventually found a job managing heating oil accounts for a local company. It only took me a few hours a day, which left me plenty of time to be home with Cathy.

Then we got the call that my mother was gravely ill. Somehow Paul scraped up enough money for me to fly home to

California to see her. She was in the hospital with severe arthritis and bleeding ulcers, and at first I really thought it would be our last visit.

Mama eventually pulled through, but it required eight months in the hospital and the loss of most of her stomach. By the time she came home, she had lost her ability to walk. This was a real blow to someone who had always done everything for everybody else. For a time she was extremely bitter. But Daddy was always there for her, loving her as much as ever, always patient, always kind.

Indeed, I have always looked back on my stepfather's conduct during this time as a prime example of Christ-like love, being willing to take up the cross, with all its pain, for the sake of the joy that lies on the other side of self-sacrifice. My stepfather never formally professed any religion. But I think he lived the Gospel message better than many of us, who claim to know the way to salvation for ourselves and others.

That was lesson number two during this trying period—God loves a cheerful giver, and He blesses those who face hardship with faith, patience, and dignity.

∽

Finally, life appeared to be settling down. I was back from California and, as my pregnancy entered the third trimester, I left my job with the heating oil company in order to prepare for the arrival of Baby Brown number three.

And what an arrival it was!

It was in the middle of the night when my water broke, which is ordinarily a sign that the onset of labor isn't far off. Remembering how quickly Cathy had been delivered, we rushed right into the hospital for what we were sure would be a speedy labor and delivery. This was on the 17th of June.

But the 18th came, the labor escalated and then dropped off, and no baby. The 19th came. Again the labor escalated. Again it dropped. Again, no baby. All this time I was in a labor room with a bunch of wires taped to my tummy, monitoring the baby's heartbeat. After three days of false starts, that heartbeat had begun to grow quite weak. The doctors—and Paul and I, as well—were starting to get worried.

It soon became clear that the baby was in distress and that immediate steps had to be taken. Fortunately, Paul and I were told, the most accomplished doctor in the area happened to be on duty that night. He would be the best person imaginable to handle the situation. We couldn't be in better hands. You guessed it—he was my old debate foe, Dr. Crosby.

At that point, I really wasn't thinking about the debate, and Dr. Crosby was far too professional to let our past encounter color his attitudes. He sized up the situation and ordered an immediate Caesarian section. I wasn't too excited about the prospect of major surgery, but after three days of labor I just wanted to get that baby born! And so, within a few minutes, I was drifting off to the happy land of anesthesia.

What I didn't realize then was just how serious the situation really was. Unbeknownst to me, Paul and Dr. Crosby were discussing the likelihood that the baby would be stillborn. Not only that, given my history of difficult childbirth, and the prolonged labor I had already endured this time around, Dr. Crosby was concerned that I might not survive, either. I can only imagine the agonies that Paul must have suffered, pacing outside that operating room, awaiting the outcome of the operation.

As it turned out, he needn't have worried. The most skilled surgeon in the state delivered Christina Lee Brown at 9:37 p.m. on June 19. We had intended to name her Nancy, but in view of all that had happened, we thought Christina was a better reflection of our gratitude to the Lord. We named her Lee in honor of the woman who had suggested, several years before, that I make the acquaintance of a Mr. Paul Brown.

Christy's birth came almost three full days since my water had broken. She was beautiful (of course!) and perfectly healthy. The only ill effect I suffered was an infection, which prevented me from holding her for five days. That was difficult, of course. But once I learned how grave the situation had been, waiting a few days to hold my baby didn't seem like such a hardship after all.

I had a fairly long recovery from Christy's birth. I spent part of my time writing to each of the hospital staff who had been so helpful to us during our long ordeal. I even wrote a letter to the editor of the local newspaper, praising Dr. Crosby's expertise. When I went in for my six-week checkup, I took Christy with me and asked Dr. Crosby if he would like to come out and see her. He looked at me in a very strange way and said, simply, "No. I can't."

I puzzled over his response for a long time. In retrospect, I suppose he must have been struggling with the conflict between his obvious talent for saving life and his conviction that it was all right to take life at the whim of the mother. Did it occur to him—as it certainly did to me—that had I been on another floor of the hospital that night, he would have been killing Christy rather than saving her?

I don't know. I never had another opportunity to talk to him. I do know that at last report Dr. Crosby was no longer doing abortions himself but was devoting much of his time to specializing in women with distressed pregnancies. I'd like to think that his experience with Christy and me had something to do with that. I still pray for him, as I do for all present and former abortionists, that their hearts may be softened.

Lesson number three: God can use times of trial to touch the hardest of hearts. Thus it was, I believe, that He used Christy and me to help Dr. Crosby move a few steps forward in his awareness of the sanctity of life.

∽

When Christy was eight months old, Paul was transferred to Steubenville, Ohio—his first job as manager of his own store. This

Hugh at five years, Cathy at three and Christy at four months.

kind of transfer typically took effect immediately, which meant that the family, in this case us, was left behind, sometimes for several weeks. Paul flew to Steubenville one Monday morning to get acquainted with his staff, take over operations at the store, and start looking for a home for us.

The very next day Christy developed a fever—a very high fever. Her temperature went up to 105 degrees. I called the pediatrician, who suggested I give her an alcohol bath. Her temperature went down for a while, but spiked again a few hours later. I gave her another alcohol bath, and her temperature went down as it had before. Unfortunately, it also went back up again. By three in the morning she was in convulsions, and I was nearly in a panic. I frantically called neighbors until I was able to borrow a car and get the other kids watched. Then I raced off to the hospital, praying all the while that Christy would be all right.

When we arrived, the emergency room staff took Christy from me, rushed her into an examining room with the doors slamming shut behind them, and didn't communicate with me again for several hours. When the doctor finally came out, his expression was grim. Christy was now in a coma. They had given her a spinal tap, fearing that she might have spinal meningitis. She might or might not survive.

Little Christy lay in her crib in the intensive-care unit for two days, with an IV in her head, without moving. I was beside myself. The worst part was that I had been unable to communicate with Paul through all this. Since we were in the process of moving, our home phone had been disconnected. I had to rely on the assistant manager of the local K-Mart store to convey messages to Paul at the Steubenville store. Though I sent several urgent messages, for some reason no one even tried to contact him until the third day, when Christy finally came out of the coma.

It happened just that suddenly, too. Three days after I had rushed her to the hospital, she woke up, her fever returned to normal, and she broke out in a bright red rash from head to toe. Her problem was not spinal meningitis, but a case of roseola measles.

Lesson number four: In our weakest moments, in the midst of our most terrible fears, when we feel most alone—even then our Lord is at our side, working His will in our lives. Without Paul there to lead me, I had to handle Christy's crisis all alone. I learned, for the first time, that I did indeed have the strength to cope with such an ordeal.

∽

By the time Paul finally got word of Christy's condition, she was already out of danger. By the time he got back to Kannapolis to be with us, I was more than ready to leave. We had weathered a great many trials there and, even though I can see how the Lord used each experience to prepare us for what lay ahead, it was still extremely difficult at the time.

There were so many tests in such a short period of time that I occasionally doubted my ability to cope. I can remember times of crying, then laughing, then crying again, wanting nothing more than to hang onto my dear husband and never let him go again. Even though we had survived it all, I never wanted to go through it again. I just wanted to tell Paul how much I loved him and how much I hoped we would never be separated again.

Chapter

Hello, Congressman!
1975–1976

Settling into our new life in Steubenville was a real challenge.

All three children became ill almost immediately upon our arrival in town, and we had no idea what was causing it. We had more coughs, more colds, and more ear infections than I ever imagined three human beings could have in the course of 12 months—which turned out to be the total length of our stay in Steubenville.

Soon after we moved into our townhouse, we set about the usual scavenger hunt, which I'm sure is familiar to anyone who has ever had to relocate because of a career. We searched out a good pediatrician, located our parish and got to know the pastor, Fr. Robert Mascolino. Hugh, who was to enter first grade, got his first Catholic school uniform and caught the bus every morning right in front of our home. Cathy and Christy shared a bedroom and got along about as well as two sisters ever do when they share a bedroom.

∽

We had been attending our new parish for about three months when a notice appeared in the bulletin announcing a pro-

Eight

I give you my word, if you are ready to believe that you will receive whatever you ask for in prayer, it shall be done for you.

Mark 11:24

life meeting. Upper Ohio Valley Right to Life was looking for new members. This was 1975, and even though the *Roe v. Wade* decision had been in force for more than two years, awareness of the reality of child-killing still had not sifted down to the grass-roots level of American life, even among Christians.

At the meeting, the leaders mentioned that they needed an editor for the newsletter. I volunteered. They also mentioned the need to identify a local business that would let them sell pro-life Christmas cards on the sidewalk. Paul offered the K-Mart store that he now managed. The card sale was a great success, and opened the way to bake sales, a flea market, and many other activities that raised much-needed funds for our group and helped us spread the word about the plight of the preborn.

I was soon chosen to represent our chapter at meetings of the Ohio Right to Life Society, which is where I met the man who really taught me how to be an articulate pro-life spokesman. I am referring, of course, to our state chairman, Dr. John C. Willke. He spoke with eloquence and ease, he emphasized the sanctity of all life and the child's right to life from the moment of conception, and he emphasized the importance of faith in doing pro-life work.

∽

In January 1976, Upper Ohio Valley Right to Life asked me to go to the March for Life in Washington, DC—it would be held on the third anniversary of *Roe*—and to represent them at a special breakfast with members of Congress.

I was thrilled, of course. I even made a new suit for myself for the occasion. I had to. Thanks to the stresses of the last couple years in Kannapolis and now in Steubenville, I had regained most of my excess weight. Our finances were also such that I had to make most of the clothes for myself and the children. I loved every minute of the sewing, especially for our dainty daughters, and was glad to be able to afford something new when a special occasion arose.

And the trip to Washington was definitely a special occasion. The day before the march, I went to a meeting sponsored by the March for Life Corporation. The president, Nellie Gray, spoke brilliantly for 40 minutes about standing for our principles, about God's blessing of new life and about our call to be soldiers in the war against innocent preborn children. That speech made such an impact on me that to this day, whenever I think of it, the same feel-

Below: Cathy, age eight months.

Right: Hugh teasing Cathy.

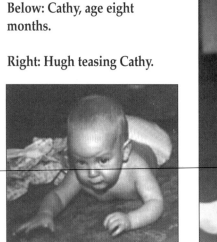

ings of excitement and resolve well up within me. I wanted to do more for the preborn. I wanted to be closer to the action. That night I prayed that our Lord would somehow make it happen. It was a fateful prayer, as I was soon to learn.

The next day I had breakfast with our Congressman, Wayne Hayes. He was getting a lot of unfavorable publicity at the time, because of his cavorting with his attractive "secretary," Elizabeth Ray. Though I was less than impressed with his commitment to family values, I had learned from my experience with Dr. Crosby that God never gives up on anyone, and I talked my head off that morning about the babies, and the need to protect them. He listened politely, then gave his political justification for doing nothing. It was a speech I was to hear many times, in many forms, from many politicians over the years.

Frustrated by my encounter with Congressman Hayes, but still invigorated by the March for Life and especially by Nellie Gray, I arrived back in Steubenville on fire for the pro-life cause. I told Paul I had prayed that he would be transferred to the Washington area. His response was immediate and emphatic: "That is the last !@#^$@ place on earth I'd ever want to live!"

Well, two weeks later Paul was transferred. Care to guess where?

Paul fussed and stewed about it, but eventually he accepted the transfer. It was a promotion, which meant more prestige within the company, more money, and better benefits. I called Dr. Willke and told him of our impending move. He promised to introduce me to Dr. Mildred Jefferson, president of the National Right to Life Committee, so that I could volunteer my time there if I wished. I then went to the Upper Ohio Valley chapter to relinquish my various responsibilities. By this time we had managed to build up an active membership, so the transfer wasn't difficult.

∽

It had been an eventful year in Steubenville—a year that launched Paul and me into pro-life work once and for all. We had learned a lot. Still, I was glad to leave. We had eventually isolated the cause of the kids' health problems in the coal dust that settled over the city every morning, but though I learned some cleaning and air-filtration techniques that made things a bit better, they still suffered. Now we stood on the brink of what we sensed would be grand adventure. I paused then, as I do now, to pay tribute to so wonderful people who cared, who sacrificed, who persisted in the efforts on behalf of the babies.

To Pauline Hoagland, whose involvement was with guile, I express gratitude for her patient, tender concern for e and every one of us who worked with her. To Guy Traversa, wh now with the Lord, I pay tribute to his efforts to lead the lc Knights of Columbus to the forefront of the pro-life effort v spiritual, financial, and physical support. I express my admirat for Susan Krantz, who struggled to speak out even as she placed needs of her own children first. And to all the others, I simply thank you for being there when it was anything but popular to pro-life in Steubenville, Ohio.

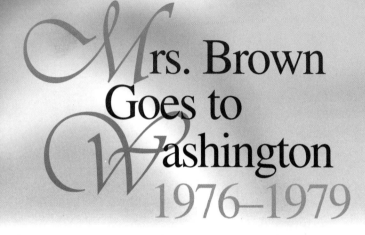

Chapter

Mrs. Brown Goes to Washington
1976–1979

We moved to Washington with the usual Brown family flair—Cathy, Christy, Hugh, and Mom (that's me) all had the chicken pox. If you are an adult who has never had the chicken pox, I don't recommend it. I really got sick. Poor Paul had to take care of everyone all by himself, right in the midst of getting settled in a new home and a new job.

In time, life got back to normal (whatever "normal" is for a crew like ours!). Paul had found a townhouse for us in Woodbridge, Virginia, about 30 miles south of Washington. Hugh and Cathy started school—Cathy was in kindergarten now—and Christy stayed home with me.

But I myself didn't stay home for long. In April 1976 I ventured into the city to visit the offices of National Right to Life, to meet with Dr. Mildred Jefferson and the rest of the staff. "The rest of the staff" turned out to be only two other people. It seemed that the executive director had left several months before and had not yet been replaced. Activity was at an all-time low. Even the remaining two women had little to do because the phones seldom rang and almost no mail came in.

Nine

Where there is jealousy and strife, there also are inconstancy and all kinds of vile behavior. Wisdom from above, by contrast, is first of all innocent. It is also peaceable, lenient, docile, rich in sympathy and the kindly deeds that are its fruits, impartial and sincere. The harvest of justice is sown in peace for those who cultivate peace.

James 3:16–18

Dr. Jefferson still had a dynamic vision of NRLC as an umbrella organization under which all the other pro-life efforts in the country could come together. And she still had a tremendous flair with the media. What she needed was someone with business experience, someone who could shape things up and get things moving and put a spark into the operation—someone like me! Before I knew it I had signed on.

On one hand, it was a dream come true. I would be able to do the thing that meant more to me than anything else in the world—help save the babies. And I would be able to do it alongside Dr. Jefferson, which would be a pleasure and an honor like no other.

On the other hand, I still had three small children, ages eight, six, and three. Until now I had considered myself a full-time, stay-at-home mom. Working full time outside the house was not what I had bargained for. But the opportunity proved too tempting to resist. I put all three kids in a private school.

It was, to say the least, stressful. I was able to carpool into the city with Paul and two others, but it meant leaving the house at 6 a.m. Believe it or not, by leaving at that ungodly hour, we were just able to arrive at our destinations by 8 a.m. We got back home at 6 p.m., after stopping to pick up the kids.

I maintained this pace for two years. During that time, we did manage to significantly enhance the effectiveness of NRLC. We expanded to 20 employees, six times the office space, and immeasurably greater national prominence. I was consumed with it. I worked at home on nights and weekends, giving over every waking hour that wasn't directly taken up with immediate family necessities. Still, looking back, I have to say it wasn't worth the price I paid by putting my vocation to the pro-life cause—important as it was—ahead of my vocation as a wife and mother.

Finally I had to scale back. The immediate reason was that we bought a new house 10 miles farther away from the city. The logistics of travel and child care, which had always been ridiculously complicated, now became simply impossible. And besides, it was time to make my own life correspond to my pro-family convictions by becoming a real wife and mother again.

I met with Dr. Jefferson and told her I was putting my kids (now 10, eight, and five) in a normal parish school and that I would be leaving the office at two o'clock every afternoon so I could be there when they got home. I was going to clean the house and do the laundry and cook dinner again. She consented without hesitation. I felt a great sense of relief.

It didn't last long. Things were changing for Paul, just as they had for me.

∽

People magazine featured Paul and me and the work of LAPAC in its January 22, 1979, issue.

Essentially, Paul was feeling that he had outgrown the opportunities available to him with K-Mart, and he wanted to get away from the pressure, the 80-hour work weeks, and the constant specter of having to pull up stakes and relocate every year or two. Like me, he longed for a more normal home life. And, like me, he wanted to do more for the babies.

A few months before, Paul had helped found something called the Life Amendment Political Action Committee, or LAPAC. Its goal was to mobilize money, manpower, and political clout against pro-abortion political candidates, and to support those who were pro-life.

The idea had come from the noble, but doomed, presidential campaign of Ellen McCormack in 1976. Paul, who was a great student of politics and a fanatic about the need for effective political action on behalf of the pro-life cause, greatly admired Mrs. McCormack and her band of dedicated supporters. They had shown how far a determined candidate could go, carrying the message of the sanctity of life and the need to defend each and every preborn child, bucking the political system, getting by on a shoestring budget. Surely, Paul thought, a national political action committee could do the same kind of thing across the country, by doing nothing more than making public where the various candidates stood on abortion.

LAPAC did indeed start on a shoestring. Its founders—Paul, Robert L. Sassone, Sr., and Morton Downey, Jr. (yes, the infamous television talk-show host)—were passionately committed

NRLC Convention Chicago, June 18, 1977.

to making a difference for the babies, but all had full-time jobs. They and their small group of volunteers were extremely limited in what they could accomplish.

But all that changed one Sunday evening when Paul went to Mass. The kids were sick and we were going to Mass on "split shifts," so Paul was by himself. When he came home, he simply announced that he was resigning his job the next morning. Without a moment's hesitation I replied, "Great!"

He later told me it was the sermon that had moved him to take such a bold step. The theme had been, "The only things of value in this life are the things you can take with you into eternity." He realized, he said, that he didn't want to retire from a company where his main achievement was keeping his toothpaste displays in order. Being a store manager, despite its prestige and good pay, was not fulfilling his desire to make his mark on the world, so that his children might have a better and more loving place to raise their families. And besides, he pointed out, America was killing one and a half million babies a year. It had to stop.

So Paul took a gamble and decided to put all his time and energy into developing LAPAC. Fundraising was the first priority, of course. In addition to backing pro-life candidates and giving the pro-life movement the political credibility it so desperately needed, he had a family to feed! But with the moral support of NRLC's board of directors—they had no political action committee of their own and were glad to see one forming—and the aid of some expert advisors, LAPAC quickly got on the move.

Its impact was felt as early as the 1978 election campaign. One of LAPAC's target races was in Iowa, where Senator Dick Clark was running for re-election. Paul had met Paul Litke earlier in the year when the young man had walked across the country, carrying a very large and heavy cross, and asking everyone he met to join with him in praying and acting against the crime of abortion. Paul remembered this young man's fervor and asked Litke if he would take up the cross again, and walk across Iowa, following pro-abortion Senator Clark everywhere he went. You see, Clark always walked his state in search of votes, but never before had he done so with a shadow like Paul Litke. The strategy worked, and Clark lost his race.

LAPAC helped defeat several additional pro-abortion senators, such as Birch Bayh of Indiana and George McGovern of South Dakota. My husband appeared on numerous national television programs, and NBC even ran a segment about LAPAC during *Weekend*, its popular news and features program. *People* magazine ran a four-page feature on Paul and Judie Brown and their three children. All in all, it was a dramatic step forward for the pro-life movement. Finally we would be taken seriously in the political arena for our ability to help elect—and defeat—candidates for office.

∽

My own world began to collapse just as Paul's was coming together. Trouble was brewing at NRLC. Some of the leadership wanted to co-opt LAPAC, bringing it under NRLC control. Paul would have none of it; he and the other board members felt that independence was a key to LAPAC's effectiveness. That led to some strained relationships at NRLC.

At the same time, I became more aware of various internal struggles at NRLC. When Dr. Jefferson left in June 1978, I realized the degree to which she had been protecting me from NRLC's officer/board politics. It was the usual sort of infighting and power struggles that occur in any organization, let alone one made up of more than 50 zealous, energetic human beings who served on the Board of Directors. But it discouraged me just the same. Paul urged me to stay on and try to make a difference. But by early 1979, it was clear to me that I simply had to leave.

In addition to the various other hassles, I found myself increasingly unable to support NRLC's views on a number of key issues. As far as I was concerned, there was no such thing as compromise when trying to save babies. That was the lesson I had learned from people such as Nellie Gray, Mildred Jefferson, Fr. Paul Marx, Dr. Murray Norris, Dr. Charles Rice and other prominent national pro-life spokesmen. But NRLC was dismayingly silent on such subjects as abortifacient birth control devices, and it endorsed a political strategy that left the door open to abortion in certain cases.

As far as I was—and am—concerned, the baby in the womb is a human being, entitled to the full rights of a human being, whether that baby has been in the womb one day or six months, and whether the result of marital union or as a result of rape or incest. That is the starting point, the fundamental reality, that must underlie all our efforts.

Thus, when we know that some birth control devices, such as the IUD, actually work by inducing early abortions, we must oppose them, period. And when we know that each and every child in the womb is a human being (and an American citizen, fully protected by the Constitution), we dare not suggest that some babies may not be worth saving—may legitimately be candidates for death—because of the circumstances of their conception. Rape and incest are unspeakably evil acts. But the baby in the womb is the victim of those acts, not the perpetrator. He or she deserves to be protected, not punished—especially when the punishment is a cruel and painful death.

We must be unflinchingly consistent in our philosophy, or we lose all credibility and moral force. Yes, politicians may have to settle for half-measures at times, out of political expediency. But you and I, who stand for nothing if not for the complete and final eradication of abortion, can never let ourselves be perceived as supportive of anything that denies the personhood of any preborn child. Personhood is our absolute. We cannot waver from it.

So, in March 1979, I resigned from NRLC.

I want to make clear that I have never viewed any individual at NRLC as being anything less than totally committed to the proposition that each and every abortion is murder and must be stopped. But I was unhappy with NRLC's strategy in pursuing its aims. I was afraid their approach would make it too easy for politicians to get away with statements such as "I am personally opposed to abortion, but. . . ." and "I am against abortion, except. . . ." To my way of thinking, then and now, there can be no "buts" and no "excepts" when it comes to saving the babies. If we retreat from our absolutes—if we start settling, philosophically, for incremental change—then our effectiveness is ended and our movement is dead.

Chapter

A Telegram From Heaven

1979–1980

It was on March 1, 1979, that I dropped my letter of resignation in the mail to NRLC. The sound of that letter hitting the bottom of the mailbox seemed to trigger the most extraordinary sequence of events I had ever experienced. It was as if the Lord had been waiting to communicate with me about what He wanted me to do next, and my leaving NRLC made that communication possible. And what a communication it was! I have always referred to the entire experience as "receiving a telegram from heaven."

Paul and I had been invited to a reception in Washington that afternoon. After mailing my resignation letter, I phoned Paul to tell him what I had just done and to tell him I was on my way to meet him. While I was driving downtown, Paul got another phone call. It was from Morton Blackwell, an associate of the conservative direct-mail fundraising guru, Richard Viguerie. He said that Mr. Viguerie was interested in providing start-up funds for a new pro-life group and was looking for someone to head up the effort. I was Mr. Viguerie's first choice, Morton said, but they knew I was loyally committed to NRLC, and wondered if we might be able to recommend someone else.

Ten

Trust in the Lord with all your heart, on your own intelligence rely not; In all your ways be mindful of him, and he will make straight your paths.

Prov. 3:5–6

Paul just laughed. "Morton," he said, "you're not going to believe this, but . . ."

∞

That is how the odyssey of American Life Lobby (dormant since 1991) and American Life League began.

Within a month I had met with Mr. Viguerie to discuss ideas, engaged an attorney to help with the paperwork, and met several times with our pro-life friends, Robert L. Sassone, Sr. and Gabrielle Avery (who has since gone to be with the Lord). Sitting around the dining room table in our home, we selected a name for our new organization; invited Gabrielle's husband, Walter, to serve as its first treasurer; and directed our lawyer to start drawing up papers for two non-profit corporations—one oriented to influencing lawmakers (American Life Lobby), the other oriented to educating the public about pro-life issues (American Life League).[1]

It took a few months to work out all the details. I stayed home during that time, helping Paul with LAPAC, caring for the children, and developing ideas for *ALL About Issues*, our organization's newsletter, which I wrote on my IBM Selectric typewriter and distributed using LAPAC's copier and addressograph machine.

I also wound up spending a fair amount of time working through some personal struggles. My last months at NRLC, and my eventual decision to leave, had been very hard on me. Some of the time I felt anger. Some of the time I felt self-pity. Almost all of the time I felt confusion. I never questioned whether I had done the right thing, but I had to deal with a lot of emotional turmoil. Finally I decided that there was simply nothing I could do about what had happened—but with God's grace, there was a great deal I could do to help other pro-life people become better soldiers for the Lord in the battle to stop the slaughter of the innocents.

By October, we were ready for our first fundraising effort. We had no mailing list of our own at all, so we had to start from scratch. The Viguerie company would rent lists of names of people they thought might be pro-life, and then simply send letters to them, describing our new organization and asking them to support it. It was slow going for a while. In those days, being the director of ALL meant that I was the one who counted the money, wrote the

Working at home on *ALL About Issues*, the organization's newsletter in its infancy.

Reviewing *ALL About Issues* in 1980 with editor Edwin Elliot, Jr.

thank-you letters, and answered the phone calls. I was the only "staff" we had!

I must say our children were quite pleased with this whole turn of events, because they got to have Mom at home all the time. I liked it, too. I knew the kids were at an age when it was important for me to be there for them, and now I was able to do that. The kids grew in their pro-life convictions, too. Even Christy, at the tender age of five, knew that abortion killed babies and was quick to say so to anyone who looked as though he needed to be told.

By the following spring—March 1980—American Life Lobby had grown to a point where it could hire two part-time staffers. This was when I really began to appreciate our community of Stafford, Virginia. We found people who were capable, committed, and more interested in saving babies than in making money (which was fortunate, since we couldn't afford to pay much). The circulation of *ALL About Issues* was growing, and we decided to publish it in a newspaper format and put it out once a month. It had always been my philosophy—and still is—that the best thing I could do to help save the babies was to arm others with the ammunition they needed to be effective in the field. Even in those early days, *ALL About Issues* was a valuable asset to thousands of people who were working to save the babies.

∽

My own thinking about pro-life work went through an important change at this time as well. I had once again regained those troublesome 80 pounds, partly from the stress of starting up a new organization and partly because I had not yet learned the importance of consistent dependence on the Lord.

To be sure, I believed that God was guiding our family, and me, and ALL. I often thought back on the extraordinary events of March 1979, when my time with NRLC ended and my time with ALL started, on the same afternoon. It was as though the Lord simply picked me up from the ashes, without the least bit of planning on my part. All I knew was that I had to be a better wife and mother, and I had to leave NRLC. I had no thought of leading a group, speaking in public (let alone on television!), or any of the other astonishing things that were about to come my way.

I did know that no single person, no single group, and no single political party was going to stop the killing. God, and God alone, would end this horrible crime if and when the people of our nation sought Him and His will for them, rather than their own convenience.

I was finally beginning to learn that we not only can but must trust in the Lord rather than in our own pitifully weak resources. You and I cannot change minds, soften hardened hearts, or prick the conscience of a nation—but our Lord can do all these things, and will do them if we but trust in Him. I was beginning to learn that I really wasn't such a smart cookie after all—but that the Lord was willing to use me anyway.

[1] People are often curious as to why we have two organizations with the same initials, similar names, and different purposes. The reason at that time was that the tax laws require that different types of organizations be incorporated separately, as donations to them are treated differently. Believe me, it would be much simpler for us if we could put all our operations under a single banner, but the IRS won't allow it. This law changed in 1990 and American Life Lobby was put on hold because American Life League was able to amend its 501 (c) 3 status to allow for a small percentage of income to be used for direct lobbying. Finally, things would not be confusing!

Chapter

We Will Never Forget You
1980–1981

We all knew that my mother's condition was steadily deteriorating. I spoke with her by phone as often as I could, as well as with my father, who told me of her diminishing ability to do even such simple things as pick up a cup of coffee.

We had already had one crisis with Mama, in 1976, at the height of the chaotic time when I was working 12-hour days at NRLC. I'd had to make two emergency trips to Southern California to be with her. She had pulled through, however, and had even been able to spend Christmas with us that year—as it turned out, the last trip she was ever to take.

Now, in the summer of 1980, Paul and I loaded up the children and made the trek to Los Angeles, wondering whether it would be our last visit with Mama. To our relief, the visit went extraordinarily well. Though Mama couldn't move without assistance, she was a joy to be with. I was glad to see her able to enjoy her grandchildren—and vice versa.

We had been back home only a few weeks when, in the fall, Daddy had a heart attack. Back to California I went. The doctors wanted to perform quadruple-bypass surgery, to which we al-

Eleven

Praised be God, the Father of our Lord Jesus Christ, the Father of mercies, and the God of all consolation! He comforts us in all our afflictions and thus enables us to comfort those who are in trouble, with the same consolation we received from him.

2 Cor. 1:3–4

agreed. My sisters and I split the time caring for Mama, and then for Daddy as well when he left the hospital. It soon became clear that Daddy was going to be fine—indeed, he would likely be in better health than he had in years—but that Mama's suffering was only going to get worse, and her situation more serious. I went back home with a heavy heart.

I decided to put my active pro-life work on the shelf for several weeks so I could devote the holidays to family concerns. Paul and I decided I should go back to California for Thanksgiving.

LAPAC had just finished a very successful "Death Valley Walk" that was designed to focus attention, just prior to the elections, on the need for prayer and fasting so truly pro-life candidates would be elected. Thirty pro-lifers joined Paul on a walk that took them from Scotty's Castle, Nevada, to downtown Las Vegas. It was a grueling 99 miles of desert plus one mile down the Las Vegas strip. But every single participant, blisters and all, was pleased to have been part of this historic event.

So, you see, we ourselves had much to be thankful for. Our own family was stable, ALL was off to a good start, and Paul had founded a management consulting firm in addition to LAPAC, which was also flourishing. The temporary absence of one house-wife from the pro-life scene was obviously not going to make a decisive difference. The opportunity to be with my parents again—to cook the Thanksgiving turkey—was a blessing beyond measure.

∽

Unfortunately, the impact on me of the various stresses of family and career was measurable, particularly around my waist. I seemed to find solace only in food. I ate Christmas candy by the pound, as well as anything else I happened to prepare, serve, or come within reach of. By the end of the year I had gained an addi-tional 20 pounds. Paul's mother, who stayed with us at Christmas, expressed concern over my weight, but I tuned her out. After all, she didn't understand the problems I was dealing with.

In early 1981 I made my first appearance on television. The show was called "A.M. Washington," hosted by Carol Randolph. I was to debate a woman from the National Abortion Rights Action League. I arrived early, wearing my best black-and-white print dress. Needless to say, I was excited.

My excitement—that is to say, my nervousness—pretty much overwhelmed whatever effectiveness I might have had. But what happened during the program was far less memorable than what happened afterward. Carol took me aside and offered me some hints on how to dress for television. A woman of 36 who

My mother was bedridden by 1980, but loved being with her grandchildren. Back left to right: Mama, Joanna, Kimberly, Christy. Front left to right: Cathy, Dana, and Hugh

carried as much weight as I did should never, ever wear a print, she said, or a short dress, or a hairdo that was high and full around the face.

In retrospect I can only confirm how right she was. I went on the air that day wearing a dress that emphasized every single pound I carried, a hairdo straight out of the '60s, and no makeup at all. I have often joked that the pro-life cause was represented in that debate by the Bride of Bozo! It was, if nothing else, a lesson in humility. I took Carol Randolph's advice and never again wore a print in public. I did not, however, lose the excess weight.

∽

Then one morning I received the phone call I had been dreading for so long. Daddy called to tell me that Mama was gravely ill and that I had better come at once if I wanted to see her alive one last time. Paul immediately called the airline, helped me pack, and drove me to the airport; my brother-in-law met me at the other end and took me straight to my parents' home. I dropped my luggage in a heap inside the front door and went immediately to my mother's bedside.

We talked for about 15 minutes. I still remember her smile and the sparkle in her beautiful brown eyes as she told me she was ready to die. She only hoped that God would forgive her for the many times she had blamed Him for her poor health.

At 4:30 the next morning, Daddy woke me up to tell me that Mama had just passed away.

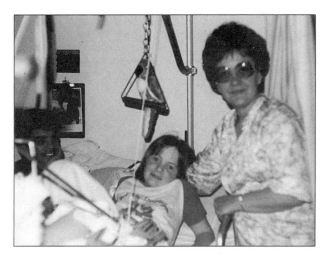

Cathy and I, bonding during her hospital stay with her leg in traction, in 1980.

The rest of the day was a blur, handling the countless details of arranging the funeral. I couldn't help but marvel at my stepfather. For 10 years he had cared for Mama, and been at her side every minute he was not at work or asleep. He made sure he came home for lunch each day to check on her. No matter what was on his mind, no matter how tired he may have been, no matter how much he might rather have been taking a break, he was always there for Mama. He brought to life for me the words of St. Paul, that God comforts us in our afflictions in order that we might be able to comfort others. He has always been for me the embodiment of the compassion we are meant to show to one another.

I wept all the way home from Los Angeles. I had lost my closest friend in the world. But I also felt relieved, knowing that Mama was at peace, without pain, and in the presence of the God she loved so dearly.

∽

I had barely recovered from the wrenching emotional ordeal of Mama's death when a new crisis hit. One Saturday morning, Christy—now seven years old—came running into the house to tell me that Cathy had fallen off her bike and was lying in the gravel.

1981: American Life Lobby presents Senator Jesse Helms with the Hero of the Year Award. Left to right: Dick Walthers, Me, Senator Helms, and Paul.

"She's dead, Mommy, she's dead!" Christy cried.

I rushed outside to find Cathy writhing on the ground, screaming in pain. By the time the ambulance had arrived, we had determined that the pain was in her leg. It turned out that she had broken her femur—the largest bone in her leg—at the hip. It was a very serious break indeed. Fortunately, one of the best orthopedic surgeons in the East was on call that day; he inserted a pin in her leg and placed her in traction. Cathy spent six weeks in the hospital wearing a full body cast, and I spent most of those six weeks at her side, trying to keep up with the mail and help Paul hold down the fort at home.

By the time Cathy came out of the hospital on crutches, I had gained yet another 20 pounds and now tipped the scales at a whopping 250! I could wear only elastic-waisted pants, and even they bulged. I told people I bought all my outfits from "Omar the Tentmaker."

In the meantime, pro-life work was enveloping our household like a giant squid. ALL now had six employees, all of whom worked in our previously unfinished basement, which Paul had had to finish just to provide some modest office space. By the end of 1980 we had more than 35,000 names on our mailing list, and the amount of work was growing just as rapidly—mail to open, requests to answer, letters to write, resource materials to compile.

In March 1981—the month Mama died—we added two more staff members. There was no more room in the basement, so we put them to work in the dining room upstairs. Paul decided that was the last straw. When things got to the point where the children felt like intruders in their own home, he said, it was time to send the pro-life movement packing. And that was just what we did. Paul bought an old, run-down building, which became ALL's new headquarters. In September we moved again, into a completely refurbished office building with space for a computer room and proper offices for the staff. Pro-life groups that had once doubted our credibility were beginning to accept the new kid on the block.

That newly won clout quickly became important to us. In October, we began to tackle something called the Hatch

Amendment. This proposed amendment to the Constitution, which was endorsed by some pro-life groups, would simply have said that the right to an abortion was not guaranteed and that all further considerations were up to the states to decide.

ALL could not accept such an amendment, which ignored the absolute personhood of every preborn child and left open the possibility that abortion might be an acceptable option. If that was the best the pro-life movement could do, we felt, we all might as well pack our bags and leave Washington. We argued, we debated, we testified, we prayed, we fasted, and in the end we defeated the Hatch Amendment.

The battle over the Hatch Amendment caused a deep division in the pro-life movement, leaving two distinct camps with two distinct ways of looking at the preborn baby. One camp said that "something was better than nothing" when it came to limiting abortion and thus was willing to accept partial solutions. ALL was—and is—totally unwilling to settle for anything less than a complete halt to the slaughter. Our view has never changed. Every life is precious and must be protected from the moment of conception.

Chapter

True Vocation
1982–1983

1982 was a year of transition for our pro-life work and for me personally. It began with the annual get-together of pro-life leaders with the president on the anniversary of the *Roe v. Wade* decision. President Reagan really invigorated us with his strongly expressed desire that abortion be stopped.

∞

But the fact of the matter was that political action in the pro-life arena was weakening, diluted by the compromising attitudes of so many leaders and groups. It had reached the point where politicians could get away with adopting the "pro-life" label merely by opposing taxpayer funding of abortion, without expressing any commitment to the absolute personhood of the preborn child.

Paul decided the time had come to step down from his position with the Life Amendment Political Action Committee (LAPAC). This was due in part to his frustration over the state of affairs in the political-action realm and in part to a desire to separate LAPAC from ALL in people's minds. In reality, the only link between the two groups was the fact that their respective directors happened to be married to each other, but people understandably

Twelve

Let hearts rejoice who search for the Lord. Seek the Lord and his strength, seek always the face of the Lord.

Psalm 105:3–4

tended to assume they were all part of the same organization. So Paul hosted the second, and last, Death Valley Walk in October of 1982 and handed over the reins of LAPAC to others.

He focused his energies on his consulting business and on serving as my chief advisor at ALL.

Our work there was continuing to expand, both in size and influence. American Life League now had more than 75,000 supporters. *ALL About Issues* had become a 48-page magazine circulated to more than 100,000 people in more than 30 countries. Though we had not yet stopped legalized abortion, I believe that we had helped save more babies by equipping people to work against abortion from the pulpit, in the classroom, and on the sidewalks in the front of the abortion clinics.

∞

Just as things were going so well, Ash Wednesday arrived—and with it a lawsuit. It had to do with a contractual dispute involving American Life Lobby and the company that was handling our direct mail fundraising. Frankly, we had grown so fast, and with so little experience at running a big organization, that we had trouble staying on top of the endless details involved in such a big operation. In time we were able to settle the lawsuit amicably, and in a way that made us stronger as an organization. But at the time it was a real blow. It had the capacity to cripple American Life Lobby and to threaten the effectiveness of American Life League, which was by far the larger of the two entities.

I did two things that Ash Wednesday in response to the lawsuit. First, I went to our lawyer. Second, I went to Mass. I felt as though this latest crisis was going to drive me over the edge unless something major happened. As it turned out, something major did happen. The Lord used the situation to bring me, at long last, fully to Himself.

It didn't start out all that "spiritual." I prayed vigorously that the Lord would help us deal with the lawsuit, and in a way that would enable both the Lobby and the League to remain in operation. I told Him that if He would help us out of the mess we were in, I would lose 100 pounds.

I know, I know. You're not supposed to make deals with

The Brown family, Christmas 1983.

God. But I didn't really think of it that way at the time. I simply had problems that were too big for me to handle, and I was asking the Lord to take charge of everything in my life—including my gluttony.

My prayers having been prayed, I set about reviewing every aspect of my life, beginning with my commitment to my vocation of being a wife and mother. I had been so moody and irritable with Paul and the kids, it was a wonder they hadn't strung me up long before. A number of things began to become clear to me.

First, as a "pro-life leader," I really thought I had all the answers and that victory would come about because of my efforts. Wrong!

I felt that my husband and children should accept the fact that pro-life work demanded most of my waking hours, including evenings and weekends, and that housekeeping, cooking, and laundry were not matters I needed to be concerned with. Wrong!

When I did prepare meals, I felt we shouldn't let anything go to waste, and that every morsel of food not consumed by someone else had to be consumed by me. Wrong!

Article appearing in *The Washington Times* on January 20, 1984.

The American Life Lobby has never wavered from the principle that each and every pre-born child is a human being, a child of God, deserving of equal protection under the law.

I felt that being in church with God once a week should be enough for anyone. Wrong—at least for me.

One by one the scales fell from my eyes. It was suddenly clear that I had to make immense changes in my life if I were ever to realize my hopes and dreams—especially my desire to one day see my mother again in heaven. I felt that the words of the book of Revelation applied to me:

> *Wake up, and strengthen what remains before it dies. I find that the sum of your deeds is less than complete in the eyes of my God.*
> *I know your deeds; I know you are neither hot nor cold. How I wish you were one or the other—hot or cold! But because you are lukewarm, neither hot nor cold, I will spew you out of my mouth!* (Rev. 3:2, 15–16).

∽

It was all too true. Clearly, I was headed straight for the condition of spiritual lukewarmness that is so offensive to our Lord.

I pose with Presidential candidate Ronald Reagan and Senator Paul Laxalt during a political gathering in early 1980.

I had become a couch potato in the vineyard of the Lord. That Lent I became acquainted, as never before, with my own need and my own faith—and with the need to nurture that faith with sincerity more than once a week on Sunday mornings.

It was a slow, painful process. It took almost a year to get down to my desired weight of 145 pounds. But with the Lord's help, I made it. I never went to a diet counselor or even a doctor. I just began taking vitamins, cooking for a family, and eating for a sparrow. What a novel experience, leaving food on the plate! When I stopped eating fat, the fat went away. Gradually I shrank from a size 24 to a size 10. My kids—now ages 13, 11, and eight—really noticed the change. The day Hugh said to me, "Mom, you really look great!" was one of the brightest of my life.

The lawsuit that had started on Ash Wednesday ended, interestingly enough, on Good Friday, when our lawyer called to say that an amicable resolution had been reached. The fundraising company took a hands-on approach to helping the Lobby retire a debt that had seemed unmanageable, and the Lobby, in turn,

I accept Pro-Life Action League Award from League Director Joe Scheidler, 1982. I testify against tax-payer funding for Planned Parenthood, as an apathetic Congressional committee listens, 1983.

became a fiscally sound organization. Thus we turned a major corner in our ability to serve those who were looking for a pro-life group that would lead, not wait; that would fight, not stand still; that would hold the line for the babies, not cut deals.

Paul never wavered in his support of me through all this. People sometimes say that marriage is a 50–50 proposition, but they couldn't be more wrong. There have been times when our marriage was a 100–0 proposition, in one direction or the other. Through each of these periods our love grew stronger, our faith grew deeper, and our ability to withstand whatever was thrown in our way became greater.

It is impossible to continue in pro-life work without strong family support and constant re-examination of priorities. I always tell people that God gave me one vocation—to be a good wife and mother. When I falter in that vocation, then nothing else in my life will bear good fruit. To be pro-life is to be pro-family, and that commitment must take concrete, tangible form in the way we live our daily lives.

The events of this hectic year finally brought me to my knees—literally, at daily Mass. Receiving the Eucharist has become the cornerstone of my relationship with the Lord.

It humbles me that I had to sink so low before I could realize how distorted my priorities were and how great my need for the Lord was. It was, of course, nothing more than what my parents had tried to teach me, what my grade school teachers had tried to model for me, and what the Lord Himself had been trying to get across to me. It had taken an almost impossible set of crises to get the message through. But now the journey of faith had begun in earnest for me, and I believe it was this that made the coming events more spectacular for me than they would have been had I not traveled this road.

Chapter

The Wilting of the White House
1983–1985

American Life League's influence began to extend farther and farther. In late 1983 we helped sponsor an international pro-life congress in Rome. This gathering was the result of meetings throughout the previous year among pro-life leaders from various organizations, who agreed that the relationship of birth control to abortion needed to be addressed more strongly.

The congress was a real watershed. Speakers came to Rome from around the world—as far away as Africa and China—and told story after story of how officials from the United States Agency for International Development had vigorously advanced the pro-abortion, pro-death agenda in their countries. Tapes of these presentations were sent to officials in the Reagan Administration. We were certain they would make an impact there.

But no. We never heard a word from anyone in the administration about the tapes, the horror stories they contained, or the congress at which they had been recounted. The silence was deafening. Was our once-staunch White House starting to wilt? Was our pro-life President starting to reveal feet of clay?

Thirteen

Politics, we were to discover, could have strange effects on people.

∞

1984 was an election year, of course. The year had long since been immortalized by George Orwell's famous novel—titled *1984*—about a society where everything was turned upside down—weakness was strength, truth was fiction, black was white. And so it was that in 1984 we actually began to see pro-life dollars being donated to the reelection campaigns of several pro-abortion Senators. Why? Because they were Republicans, and it was considered important to retain a Republican majority in the Senate. No one ever seemed to stop and ask why a Republican majority was so important if the Republicans in question were not willing to support measures that would protect preborn babies.

1984 was also the year of a major international meeting in Mexico City. The meeting was to address the topic of world population. Policymakers from governments around the world would be there. The aim of the meeting was to help disadvantaged nations address the economic problems caused by overpopulation.

It didn't take a genius to figure out what the agenda of many of those policymakers would likely be. They would press for greater use of birth control and abortion, rather than addressing the real needs of families. We decided we needed a way to influence the meeting directly. We no longer felt we could trust the White House, where the "wilting" on pro-life issues was now almost complete.

So our staff personally collected and collated the material we thought the delegates ought to see, and sent a team to Mexico City to hand-deliver it. Former U.S. Senator James Buckley, a strong pro-lifer who was part of the U.S. delegation, helped us get the material into the right hands. It was also Mr. Buckley who announced, a few days later, that the United States would deny support to any government that used coercive family-planning methods or that utilized abortion as a means of birth control. Mild as that policy was, it still sent shivers down the spine of the pro-death groups—which was precisely our intent.

∽

1985 came, and with it the annual meeting of pro-life leaders with the president. That meeting changed my attitude toward politics, and politicians, forever.

The invitation for the meeting came via telephone, as was customary. In this case, the call came from the man who was the White House liaison for social policy affairs. The invitation was to both Paul and me—me because of ALL, Paul because of his political acumen and his experience with LAPAC.

Paul and me with President Reagan, 1982.

To Judy and Paul Brown
With appreciation and best wishes, Sincerely,
Ronald Reagan

In order to understand what happened, you need to know that these kinds of meetings with the president are always carefully prepared, almost scripted. Those invited to the meeting propose topics to be discussed, which are assembled into a briefing book. The president's staff reviews the contents of the book with him, so that he will be able to engage the issues without spending a lot of time on background information. The participants, for their part, decide ahead of time who will address which segment of the book, to avoid duplication of effort and to make sure all the main points get covered.

When the White House representative asked me which topic I wanted to address, I was able to respond immediately. We were facing a new threat, I told him—the entrance into our research centers of a drug called RU-486, which was designed to induce "do-it-yourself" abortions through the tenth week of pregnancy. It was imperative, I said, that federal funding of research on RU-486 be stopped, and that Food and Drug Administration approval of it be denied. I felt that the president could play an important role in this.

I was astonished by the man's response. RU-486 was not in the briefing book, he said. Therefore, the president would not be prepared to discuss it fruitfully. Therefore, I was not to bring it up at the meeting under any circumstances. After all, we did not want to embarrass the president.

Well, it seemed to Paul and me that if the president was unaware of what RU-486 was, and of the fact that his own government was sponsoring its development, then he needed to know about it, whether it was embarrassing or not. Most of the embarrassment, I suspected, would be on the part of those White House aides who seemed to be keeping the president in the dark on this crucial matter.

So when my turn came to speak at the meeting, I told President Reagan everything about the RU-486 "death pill." I handed him copies of research grants that the government was sponsoring, along with a book that had recently been released by those who supported the drug, and pleaded with him to stop the funding. He seemed amazed, though not particularly embarrassed. He asked me several questions and assured me that action would be forthcoming.

Paul, for his part, also launched into a topic that wasn't "in the book." He told the stories of several pro-life activists who had been given extraordinarily harsh jail sentences for a variety of alleged offenses. Couldn't the White House review these cases, he asked, and look into getting the sentences reduced or even remitted? The president said he was unaware that such cases existed and promised to look into the matter.

History shows that the White House never did move to block the funding of research on RU-486, and did next to nothing about the pro-lifers who had been so unjustly treated by the courts. It was the clearest indication to date—as if any more indication were needed—of the wilting of the White House. For while President Reagan remained committed to a pro-life America, he was surrounded by staffers and advisors who either did not share his position or considered it not a high priority. Indeed, we later learned that there were people in the administration who worked without ceasing to block action on any of the suggestions made during our brief meetings with the president. I—and perhaps most of the other leaders—was simply too naive to realize it at the time.

The only concrete result of that particular afternoon was that Paul and I were told we would never be invited back to the White House again. We felt vindicated, somehow. Had we acquiesced to the order to remain silent, had we gone along with the "briefing book game," we would have been untrue to our principles, to the babies, to our Lord. If we were going to offend someone, we decided, then White House staffers were the ones to offend, not the Lord.

Chapter

If I Should Die Before I Wake

1985

1985 was the year of some of ALL's greatest advances, and of one of the most harrowing crises of my life.

The nature of the pro-life struggle began to shift with the entry into the discussion of what were called "school-based clinics," or SBCs. The idea seemed simple, and innocent, enough—clinics located inside grammar schools, junior high schools, and senior high schools, where children could receive needed medical attention and counseling free of charge. Sounds great, doesn't it?

But we began to smell a rat when we saw the names of the people who were advocating SBCs. There was Douglas Kirby, a former official of the Centers for Disease Control (a federal agency) in Atlanta, who was a leading advocate of expanded sex education in the schools. He was also a proponent of providing birth control advice (and devices), as well as abortion referrals, either in the schools or in clinics located nearby.

There was also Joy Dryfoos, a researcher whose articles appeared regularly in *Family Planning Perspectives*, published by the Alan Guttmacher Institute, which is the research arm of Planned

Fourteen

"Peace" is my farewell to you, my peace is my gift to you; I do not give it to you as the world gives peace. Do not be distressed or fearful.

John 14:27

Parenthood. She became very vocal about the sad reality of rising teen pregnancy, which she attributed to a lack of adequate sex education in the schools.

Somehow, with people like this involved, we suspected that SBCs had an agenda beyond treating head colds and upset stomachs. And we were right: As the SBC movement picked up speed, it became clear that the primary purpose of the clinics was to advance the pro-birth control, pro-abortion agenda. There are documented cases of students going into such clinics for something as simple as an aspirin, only to be asked to complete a survey including intimate questions about sexual behavior. The follow-up to this, of course, is an offer of birth control and abortion referral services to any students who might "need" them.

American Life League had produced many educational booklets about the relationship among birth control, promiscuity, and abortion, which had won the support of pro-life organizations from all church backgrounds. So when we went into battle against school-based clinics, we started with a solid reputation for our research and expertise. Many television and radio interviews and debates resulted. I've always been grateful to the Lord for the way we were able to spearhead what became a broad-based struggle to stop the spread of this new assault on our children.

∾

1985 was also the year I was called on to debate Faye Wattleton, the president of Planned Parenthood, on the Phil Donahue show. I was so nervous about the broadcast—the first one I had done "thin"—that I nearly became ill. I decided to go to Mass the morning of the show at St. Patrick's Cathedral in New York. I really wasn't concerned so much about embarrassing myself, but I didn't want to say anything that would betray my faith and reliance on the Lord.

I took it as a sign of special favor from the Lord that Cardinal John O'Connor himself was the celebrant that morning. He was, and is, my hero. The point of his brief homily was that when we are in distress, we must give our problems to God with faith and hope. I knew this was the Lord's way of telling me not to worry. And indeed, the show went very well.

We debated RU-486. It was astonishing how candid and matter-of-fact Ms. Wattleton was in describing how the chemical could kill preborn babies through the tenth week of pregnancy, and how energetic the audience was in its appreciation of such efficient killing

Me, recuperating at home after my surgery, 1985.

It seemed to me that Phil Donahue gave me more than my share of the time, perhaps hoping to balance things out a bit. Still, when I expressed support for chastity outside of marriage and fidelity in marriage, I thought Phil would have to have his jaw scraped off the floor. I felt utterly calm and at peace throughout the entire program. I knew the Holy Spirit was there, protecting me and guiding my tongue.

Then, in July, my world seemed to come crashing down around me.

∽

It began with three days of hemorrhaging and a trip to the gynecologist. She gave me a D-and-C, then told me that her examination had indicated the presence of a possibly cancerous growth in my left ovary. A radical hysterectomy was necessary, she said, and the sooner the better. She referred me to a group of specialists at Georgetown University Hospital.

This was serious news indeed. There are many kinds of cancer, some more dangerous than others. Ovarian cancer can be one of the most dangerous of all. I went through a battery of tests at Georgetown, all of which confirmed the original diagnosis.

The doctors wanted to operate right away. There was only one problem: Paul and I had finally been able to plan a vacation together—the first one we'd had in many years—and we didn't want to miss out on it now. We had planned to cover more than 3,000 miles driving and to be gone about three weeks.

The doctor sat quietly for a moment, then said, "Go ahead. Three weeks won't make that much difference. Either it's already gone too far, or we've caught it in time, or we're just plain wrong about it being cancer in the first place. So don't worry, just have a good time." Paul and I looked at each other and decided that we would have a good time. And we did. It was one of the most memorable and enjoyable trips we ever made.

The day before I went into the hospital, we invited a priest to come to the house for dinner. I had asked him to say Mass for our family, administer the sacrament of the Anointing of the Sick to me, and talk to the children about how to place their trust in the Lord. Naturally, it was very hard for the children—now ages 16, 14, and

11—to face the fact that I might die. But it was something I wanted them to be able to deal with in a spiritual way. If I did leave them, I wanted them to have confidence that God had a perfect plan for me, and for them as well.

The next morning I said goodbye to Paul, in case I didn't get the chance to speak to him later, and assured him that everything would be okay. I learned later that while he sat in the waiting room during my surgery, he happened to pick up an article about the high number of women who die from ovarian cancer. It really tore him up. I was glad to have the opportunity to hear about it and to be able to share with him my philosophy about death. How important it is to be spiritually prepared to die! How fortunate I felt to have had several weeks in which to make those preparations!

Me with Father Paul Marx, O.S.B, at the Rome (PLAN) Conference, 1984.

Walter Harrington wrote a great piece for the babies in *The Washington Post Magazine* **about this woman who traveled around the country speaking about chastity, preborn babies and birth control.**

As things turned out, I did indeed have cancer cells in my ovary. Twenty-one separate biopsies were performed. But the operation was a success. All the cancerous cells were removed. I never needed any follow-up radiation or chemotherapy. To this day— praise God!—I remain cancer free.

∽

The doctor prescribed six full weeks of bed rest for my recuperation. I complied fully with everything he told me to do— not because I'm such a cooperative person by nature, but because Paul hovered over me like a mother hen, making sure I behaved myself. I was not allowed to get up from the couch for any but the most pressing reasons. You would have thought I was his child, not his wife. But that is the way Paul is—so warm and sincere in his love—and I am grateful to God for such a husband.

Still, we did occasionally have things to work out. I remember one Friday night about a week after the operation. Paul was going up to the high school to watch our son's football game. Then he told me he planned to have two women come over and baby-sit me. I begged and pleaded to be left alone. I promised to be a good girl and stay on the couch. In the end, Paul relented and cancelled the "baby-sitters." What a relief, to have an evening of peace and quiet, all to myself!

Six weeks to the day after the operation, I met with a reporter from *The Washington Post* who wanted to do a story about me for the paper's Sunday magazine. I had to chuckle at the timing. I thought to myself, "Thank you, Lord, for loving me so much, and for allowing me to be used by you on this earth, whether it's for days or months or years to come."

Then on January 22, 1986, the paper arrived with a full-color picture of me on the cover of the magazine and a wonderful story about this woman who traveled around the country speaking about chastity, preborn babies, and birth control. Though the writer, Walt Harrington, had the chance to flay me, he wrote a great piece for the babies. He wrote about pro-lifers in a positive way. I hope it affected him, and many of his readers, in some small way, so they can better appreciate the battle we are fighting and the sincerity of our efforts.

Chapter

On the Field, in the Courts, at the Polls

1986–1988

"Hey!" exclaims Paul Brown to Judie Brown. "Did you know that Tommy Herr is one of our donors? How about that? Tommy Herr!"

"Yeah, how about that," says Judie Brown to Paul Brown. "So who's Tommy Herr?"

So much for my knowledge of professional athletes.

Tommy Herr, it turned out, was the second-baseman for the St. Louis Cardinals at the time, renowned for his prowess both in the field and at the plate. It also turned out that he was pro-life and that he liked American Life League enough to support us financially.

Learning that Tommy was one of our supporters immediately revitalized an old idea, that we start a group called "Athletes for Life." Another professional baseball player, Chris Speier, had tried to form such a group a few years before, but it had not gotten off the ground for a variety of reasons. Apparently the timing just hadn't been right in the Lord's plan.

But was the timing right now? One of our staff members contacted Tommy, who responded enthusiastically. Tommy so obviously loves the Lord and His word that he was perfect for the

Fifteen

"Those who love your law have great peace, and for them there is no stumbling block.

Psalm 119:165

leadership role. As chairman of Athletes for Life, he was able to enroll many of his fellow ballplayers. He also appeared in a number of televised public service announcements, telling the American public the truth about the high failure rate of condoms and that there was a foolproof way to prevent the transmission of AIDS through sexual contact—chastity. He was terrific.

The idea grew from there. Before long Mark Bavaro, the All-Pro tight end for the New York Giants, became co-chairman of Athletes for Life and started signing up professional football players as well. He even went to the first Operation Rescue event in New York City as an observer and wound up in the paddy wagon. Athletes for Life has been extremely effective in carrying the pro-life message to the public, and especially to young people.

∽

Speaking of Operation Rescue, I participated in a rescue that year as well. One of my favorite priests, Fr. James Buckley, told me he was going to participate and urged me to join him. So one Saturday morning I drove to Fairfax, Virginia, to join a group of rescuers bent on closing down a local abortion clinic.

It was an experience I'll never forget. We were all gathered on the sidewalk when the signal came to move into place in front of the clinic's doors. Everyone around me began moving. I had planned to join them. I lifted my right foot to take a step forward, and then simply got stuck. I can't explain it, but it felt as though my feet were literally riveted to the ground. I tried to move, but I absolutely could not do so. The rescue took place with me standing there, praying my Rosary, still frozen to the sidewalk.

There are many charisms and callings, as Cardinal O'Connor so frequently reminds us, and I was beginning to realize that perhaps participating in Operation Rescue was not one of mine. I applaud the valiant efforts of those who literally stand in the way of the slaughter, but it does not appear to be my calling.

ALL was influenced by the rescue movement, though, in an unexpected and unwelcome way. In 1987, with Operation Rescue rolling across the country like a freight train, the abortion

Athletes for Life, begun in 1978, and carried forward in 1985 by American Life League, provides pro-life athletes with information and fellowship. Right: Mike Ditka, below (LtoR): George Martin, Fr. Kenneth Moore, O.Corm., Wellington Mara, Mark Bavaro.

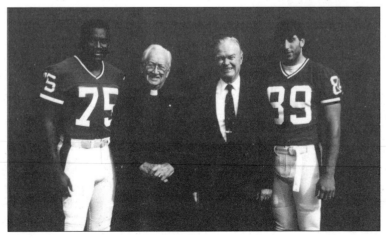

lobby came up with a new legal strategy—taking pro-lifers to court under a law designed to deal with organized crime. The law is called the RICO act, because of its stated goal of stopping Racketeer Influenced and Corrupt Organizations. The abortionists argued that Rescue's orchestrated attempts to close down abortion clinics violated this statute. And even though ALL was not formally aligned with Operation Rescue, we were hit with a RICO lawsuit just the same.

It wasn't until 1989—after a lot of anxiety and a fortune in legal fees—that we were finally free of the case. Nothing really came of it except for a couple years of legal maneuvering. Yet the travesty of the RICO act continues. It is appalling that those who kill babies are able to go about their business under the protection of the law, while those who sacrifice so much to intervene on behalf of innocent preborn babies go to jail—as gangsters, no less!

I believe the history books will one day honor these courageous men and women who put their lives on the line for the sake of the babies,

My one and only appearance on "Donahue" (Jan. 13, 1985) pitted me against Faye Wattleton, then President of Planned Parenthood; a physician; an audience; and Phil. The subject: abortion pill RU-486.

in an effort to awaken a slumbering nation to the horror of abortion.

I also believe that those who pray—for the preborn, for their mothers, and for their killers—are every bit as courageous, and every bit as effective, as those who intervene physically. Each of us has his own gift, and his own calling, from the Lord. He does not expect us to do what He has called others to do, only what He has called us to do. I believe He sees each and every aspect of pro-life work as His own love in action on behalf of the little ones. Whether or not we make the history books here on earth, we will all be included in the book our Lord is keeping!

∽

As the 1988 Presidential election rolled around, American Life Lobby received many letters from supporters, wondering how we planned to work for the Bush campaign and how they could join in. A lot of these people were angry—and more than a few stopped contributing—when we told them that we did not plan to do anything for the Bush campaign.

The reason was simple. Our board of directors, as well as all our legal and medical advisors, were unanimous in their conviction

1988 took me out to the states for speeches and to America through television interviews in my office.

that protection of the child in the womb had to be absolute. As far as we were concerned, any candidate who wanted to wear the pro-life label had to be unequivocally committed to the principle that all the babies had to be protected, not just some of them. So when George Bush went on record as saying he opposed abortion except in cases of rape, incest, or to save the life of the mother, it was clear that we could not endorse him—even though his opponent, Michael Dukakis, was far worse.

The state of pro-life political action had been deteriorating for some time and became especially troublesome in 1988. More and more candidates were trying to endear themselves to the pro-life movement by mouthing weak, equivocal statements. And more and more pro-life people were buying the argument that "something" was better than "nothing." The result was that the political clout of the pro-life movement had been severely diluted. ALL's position was clear and uncompromising: We would give no endorsement to any candidate who did not stand four-square for the principle of personhood—for equal protection for all the babies.

The only bright spot of 1988 was Pat Robertson. He campaigned on the truth of what Planned Parenthood really stood for.

1988 also took me to Congress to point out the plight of preborn children and their mothers as victims of abortion.

He pointed out that the group's founder, Margaret Sanger, had been a racist. And he spoke forthrightly about how abortion was tearing at the heart of our nation. I believe strongly that if all pro-life leaders had put their full support behind Pat Robertson, we could at least have forced George Bush to adopt a more acceptable position. But it was not to be. Our movement failed to stand firm for the truth. Instead we built a stumbling block and fell over it ourselves.

Our opponents, of course, did not make this mistake. They did not give an inch to anyone. They wanted abortion on demand, right now, period. Their unbending insistence on the woman's "right" to "choose" easily overcame the pro-life movement's tepid stand of "no killing—except under certain circumstances."

Dr. Bernard Nathanson, the former abortionist who later converted to the pro-life cause, points out that the pro-abortion forces have long been able to take advantage of compromise and disunity among pro-lifers. One of the main strategies of the National Abortion Rights Action League (NARAL), of which Dr. Nathanson was a founder, from its inception, was to stand solidly for its demands in the face of disunity and waffling from the churches and the pro-life groups. In particular, he said, it had taken advantage of disunity among the Roman Catholic hierarchy, working in various ways to drive the wedge in deeper.

It had worked as early as 1973, and it was still working in 1988. The pro-abortionists held fast to their cardinal principles while we shied away from our own. The tragedy of the "strategic," "something-is-better-than-nothing" approach is that babies die as a result. Would that we were more concerned with standing firm for God's truth than we are with finding acceptance in the halls of secular power!

Chapter

Matters of Opinion

1989

Christy was the center of my life during 1989.

In most ways, the Brown family was doing great. Hugh was playing football at the University of Maryland—an experience that only the mother of a football player could possibly understand. Cathy had begun her studies at George Mason University. Paul's business had grown and prospered. His plant was now printing most of ALL's publications, and he himself was managing the organization's finances, so we could maximize the value of each and every penny donated by our 250,000 supporters.

The only cloud on the horizon was Christy. She was still at home. And she was ill. The problem was that no one could figure out the nature of her illness. She suffered severe chest and abdominal pain, which totally debilitated her every time it flared up. We went to doctor after doctor, who put Christy through test after test, only to come back shrugging their shoulders and shaking their heads.

Fortunately, ALL now had a staff in place that did not require my physical presence in the office very much, as long as the telephone system kept operating, so I was able to stay home with Christy whenever she needed me. That was a great blessing—a

Sixteen

I have come in my Father's name, yet you do not accept me. But let someone come in his own name and him you will accept. How can people like you believe, when you accept praise from one another yet do not seek the glory that comes from the One God?

John 5:37–38

blessing for which I thanked the Lord often.

∞

In the midst of our Christy's troubles, we began to face a another dilemma on the pro-life front. It had to do with a Supreme Court case known as *Webster v. Reproductive Health Services*. It was one of the most closely watched abortion-related cases in many years.

William Webster was attorney general for the state of Missouri, whose restrictions on abortion were among the most stringent in the nation. Reproductive Health Services was a large abortion clinic in St. Louis. It had gone to court seeking to overturn the state's strict regulations. It is a legal convention that when you take a state to court, the case is listed under the name of the attorney general. Hence this particular case became known, for short, as the *Webster* case.

Webster offered a fairly straightforward choice between two basic points of view. One view held that states had the right to regulate abortion. The other held that no one could deprive a woman of her right to kill her preborn child. The decision, handed down on July 3, was a strong affirmation of the states' right to regulate abortion and thus a victory for the pro-life cause. But to turn an old saying around, this particular silver lining had a large, black cloud attached.

In its opinion, the court said that state legislatures had the right to assert that human life begins at the point of fertilization if they believed that to be the case. This, in fact, was the basis on which the Missouri law was written. The court did not say whether such a position was right or wrong, merely that states could assert it if they chose. Thus the court adopted one of the wimpiest, trendiest positions imaginable—"it's true for you if you believe it"—and applied it to one of the most pressing issues imaginable—the definition of when human life begins. In effect, it made the personhood of the preborn child a matter of opinion—and of political horse-trading.

ALL applauded the *Webster* decision as a step in the right direction, but not a very big step. It left unresolved the fundamental issue of personhood. Worse, it clouded this vital issue in the minds of many people, including many pro-life people. I had the opportunity to appear on the Oprah Winfrey Show with Molly Yard, who was then president of the National Organization for Women, and make clear ALL's unswerving commitment to the personhood of all preborn children.

∾

In August, American Life League held an educational seminar in St. Louis to discuss the *Webster* decision and where to go next in light of it. Brian Young of our staff had drafted 10 different legislative proposals that could be advanced in state legislatures. Each of the proposals was in line with the provisions of *Webster*, meaning that it should hold up in court. Each one was based on affirming the principle of personhood. Each one offered legislators an opportunity to cripple the abortion industry, address the RU-486 problem, or provide new protection for the preborn child. More than 200 people attended the seminar. It was a great opportunity to discuss the issues, debate the proposals, and work toward a united position.

One group that did not attend—though they had been cordially invited—was the National Right to Life Committee. It turned out NRLC had its own legislative proposal, which it unveiled at a small conference in Washington, DC, in October. Their proposal was based on extensive polling data, which indicated that while the vast majority of Americans were opposed to abortion as a means of birth control, many thought abortion should be permitted in cases of rape, incest, fetal deformity, and serious threat to the health of the mother. NRLC had drafted a legislative proposal embodying this poll data and planned to launch it in all 50 states.

I was disappointed with the NRLC proposal, for several reasons. The most obvious, of course, was that it failed utterly at the key point of the battle. By allowing for certain "exceptions," it undermined the principle of personhood, saying in effect that it was sometimes okay to kill babies.

I was also saddened that NRLC had chosen to bypass our August meeting and to unveil its proposal without inviting scrutiny from other groups and organizations. Once again, the pro-life movement was seen to be heading off in different directions. The press pounced on this disunity, weakening the strength of the overall movement. It also pounced on NRLC's proposed exceptions to an outright ban on abortion, correctly seeing this as an accommodation to the pro-abortion forces.

For me, it was a sad turn of events. Had we simply given up on the principle of personhood? Were we really going to settle for protecting only some babies? Were we really going to be the ones to tell lawmakers which babies should be protected—and which babies it was okay to kill?

I know, I know. Compromise is the essence of politics, and pro-life political action is therefore bound to involve compromises. I accept this. I just think it is the politicians, not the pro-lifers, who should be doing the compromising. A legislator often goes into a battle knowing, and aiming for, what he most wants. Then, along the way, he may have to give up some of what he wants in order to get some of what he wants. That is the way Congress and state legislatures work.

But it is one thing when a politician compromises on financing a new highway. It is quite another when he compromises on something that means the life or the death of innocent babies Moreover, it is one thing when a politician compromises on ar issue. It is quite another when the people committed to one side of that issue do the compromising for him. You can bet that lobbyists in other fields don't go to politicians and suggest ways in which their own interests can be undermined. Why, then, should we?

Suppose that after months of discussion and debate, a state legislator comes to ALL and says, "Look, I know you want to stop all abortions. But I can only carry this bill right now if I allow for some exceptions. I'd rather get something than nothing." Our response is simply, "We will applaud whatever gains you make. But we still won't be satisfied with anything less than a complete ban After all, every abortion kills a human being. If you feel you have to compromise, that is your decision. But we won't compromise our principles."

That is very different than our walking into the legislator's office and saying, "Well, we'd really like to save all the babies. But it's okay with us if you let abortionists kill babies from the following categories. . . ." When we do this we make a mockery of our principles, and we undermine our own effectiveness as lobbyists Politicians are already adept at compromising our principles—they don't need us to do it for them. That is why ALL will always hold firmly to the absolute need to recognize and protect the personhood of each and every preborn child.

In 1989, the *Webster* decision brought me face to face with Molly Yard, then President of NOW, on the Oprah Winfrey show.

The crowning achievement of 1989 for ALL was the production of Champions For Life, a video starring six members of the 1987 Super Bowl Champion New York Giants. The video was made possible by the generosity of Mr. Wellington Mara, co-owner of the team. It was a tremendous success, something that could touch the hearts of young people in a new and exciting way. After all these years we finally had a tool to sway the teenager or college student who didn't want to buy the phony "pro-choice" arguments.

As the year drew to a close, I found myself praying more and more that we would not let ourselves be swayed either by the disappointments of politics and by our own human frailty, or by the fleeting pleasures of momentary success. It is so easy to get caught up in the excitement of a television appearance, an appointment with a prominent government leader, or an ovation at a speech.

Whether in the face of failure or success, we need humility. In less time than we'd like to think, we will be gone and our deeds—even our names—forgotten. All that counts is whether we have faithfully done what our Lord has asked of us. He will never forget us.

∽

Daddy had a major heart attack barely a week before Christmas. We had planned a traditional family Christmas at home—both Hugh and Cathy would be home from school—but those plans had to change. Because Christy was still suffering from her as-yet-undiagnosed illness, I decided to take her with me. Off we went to California.

The situation was worse than I had anticipated. Daddy's condition was quite serious, the doctors said. There was only one heart surgeon in the West who could perform the surgery he needed—and even then it was far from clear that Daddy would be strong enough to survive. The rest of the family flew out to join us. Daddy went into surgery on Christmas Eve.

I went to Mass and spent most of the day in the chapel praying. Tears streamed down my face as I gave my stepfather over to the Lord. I tried to pray simply that God's will be done. I knew it wasn't right to try to tell God what to do. But, I must confess, much of my praying probably sounded like precisely that.

Daddy survived the emergency quadruple-bypass surgery. But he was hanging on by a thread. The physician spoke with my sisters and me that night, and again on Christmas Day. He was not very encouraging. For days, Daddy lay in an intensive-care unit, hooked up to what seemed like dozens of monitors, machines, and feeding devices. If he did not show marked improvement soon, the doctor said, his chances of survival would become virtually nil.

Our prayers became increasingly urgent. Here lay a man, only 64 years old, who had given himself to our mother so unselfishly for so long, and who had poured himself out for us as well. The thought of losing him was more than we could bear.

Almost miraculously, it seemed, his condition began to improve. Within a few days he was unhooked from most of the machines. By the time we returned home he was smiling, happy, and in full control of the situation. His biggest concern was whether or not he would be allowed to drive his car.

None of us had ever received a better Christmas present. All we could say was, "Thank you, Lord, for loving Daddy, and for allowing us to have him with us a little while longer."

Chapter

**Betrayal
and Unity**
1990

Sometimes things happen where you least expect them. Who would have imagined that after years of conflict, debate, and activity in places like Washington, DC, and New York, the pro-life controversy of the year would erupt in Idaho?

But that is exactly what happened. I suppose I shouldn't have been surprised. As I continued to attend daily Mass, I was becoming overwhelmed by the truth of the lessons I was reading in *The Imitation of Christ*, a spiritual classic that I think is "must" reading for everyone who is trying to serve the Lord. The closer I grew to the Lord in prayer and in the Eucharist, the more it became clear to me that those who follow him will share in his trials and sufferings. What happened in Idaho definitely fit the mold.

The model legislation prepared by the National Right to Life Committee—the one that would restrict abortion while making exceptions in cases of rape, incest, and so on—had been passed in the Idaho legislature and now lay on the desk of Governor Cecil Andrus, awaiting his signature. Governor Andrus was thought to be pro-life. He had said previously that he would sign a bill limiting abortion as long as it contained the familiar array of "exceptions." Now, such a bill lay before him. It needed only a stroke of his pen

Seventeen

Justice will bring about peace; right will produce calm and security.

Isa. 32:17

to become the strictest anti-abortion law in the nation.

But in the end, he failed. Rather than keep his word, he vetoed the very bill he had said would satisfy him. I can't say I was completely surprised. Betrayal is in the very nature of politicians. We pro-lifers had been led on, and then let down, many times before. But there were many angry, broken-hearted people left in the wake of the governor's duplicity.

Our American Life League affiliate in Idaho was angry with the Idaho legislature. One of ALL's pieces of model legislation had been put forward for consideration but had been passed over without a second glance. Our bill would have at least forced some debate on the fundamental principle of personhood for all preborn children. Given the governor's subsequent actions, it is unlikely it would have passed. But as it was, the legislature simply opted for the NRLC proposal, laden as it was with exceptions, and the principle of personhood never even got discussed.

Moreover, the pro-life movement in Idaho was badly split by the whole affair. Some had supported the NRLC bill. Others had insisted on the need to provoke discussion of personhood. In the end, neither camp got what it wanted. I have often wondered why all the pro-life groups didn't sit down together right at the beginning and work through their differences before any bill was introduced. Maybe together they could have seen through the governor's hypocrisy in calling for a bill he later refused to sign.

All in all, the Idaho fiasco represented the tragic waste of a golden opportunity to force the bedrock issue of personhood into the light of day.

∾

As it happened, the Idaho veto came at almost the precise moment we were finally discovering the cause of our daughter Christy's pain. We had been to more than a dozen doctors over the course of more than a year. Christy had become so weak that she couldn't even go to school; I was teaching her at home. So when her latest doctor explained that she had an enlarged colon—about three times normal size—and said he wanted to perform surgery to pare it down to size, we consulted two other doctors for corroborating diagnoses, and then agreed to the operation. Christy was in the hospital for less than a week. Four weeks after the operation she celebrated her 16th birthday, and she has been fine ever since.

∾

Unity 90 featured more than 60 speakers, including (clockwise) Congressman Henry Hyde (R-IL); Cardinal John O'Connor with me; Csaba Vedlik, Lobbyist, American Life Lobby; Mildred F. Jefferson, M.D., President, Right to Life Crusade.

ALL's major event of the year was the pro-life show of shows, called "Unity 90." We hosted a four-day conference in Chicago with representatives from virtually every major pro-life organization. We also broadcast a three-hour video conference that was beamed to more than 250 locations across North America and was seen by millions of people. It was so wonderful, I can only urge you to get the video and see it for yourself.

Judge Bork was there—the one so cruelly abused by the Senate during his Supreme Court confirmation hearings—along with other major pro-life leaders, such as Cardinal O'Connor of New York, Dr. Jerry Falwell, Dr. Mildred Jefferson—my old mentor from the early days at NRLC—Dr. Bernard Nathanson, and many others.

And for three hours of the evening of Saturday, June 30, Americans got the chance to see how respectable, how caring, and how dedicated the pro-life movement is. There were compelling guest appearances by Chicago Bears football coach Mike Ditka and rape victim Kay Zibolsky. Rev. Wilbur Lane, 88 years old and completely blind, received our "Hero of the Year" award.

When the dust settled and the mail began to pour in, we learned that Unity 90 had helped spur the formation of several new

1990: Mr. and Mrs. Bart Gaffney of New York visit me at our offices; I visit Senator Jesse Helms to present him with a gift for him and his wife.

pro-life groups, including one for policemen called Officers for Life, had played a direct role in saving the lives of at least three babies, had re-invigorated many pro-lifers suffering discouragement after many years "in the trenches," and had given witness to the reality of pro-lifers being committed to God first of all, and then to the rights of the innocent, whether in the womb or in the nursery, whether in good health or bad, without exception.

∞

Unity 90 was a great success—and it nearly destroyed us! After it was over, we went into a financial tailspin. I kept telling people it was all part of God's plan; that he wouldn't have brought us this far down the road just to shove us over a cliff.

And indeed the trials and tribulations did work out to our ultimate benefit. For the first time in our history, a group of businessmen came forward and offered to form a "kitchen cabinet," a group of advisors who could guide us out of our current dilemma and help us with our financial decisions in the future. These men, who are still with us today, are like a crown of precious jewels on the head of the pro-life movement. The rest of us have been so busy fighting the fight that we have never really learned about budgets, cash-flow statements, and the other things that credible organizations need. We deeply appreciate the gift of their time and expertise—and trust it is but the beginning of a groundswell of corporate support of the pro-life movement.

Chapter

Verbal Fog
1991–1992

Balancing the corporate structure and solid fiscal growth of American Life League against the needs of the ever-changing culture became a great challenge for me during the ensuing two years. There seemed to be an ever-growing attitude in the politics-first segment of the pro-life movement that we were somehow wedded to the Republican Party. This was a disaster because it meant that the possibility of proposing truly pro-life legislation was scoffed at because it would make things difficult and uncomfortable for our so-called friends in elected positions. And besides, the polls had to be taken into account! Please let me be clear on this point—this did not deter American Life League from supporting only those legislative measures which did not allow for exceptions or other life-diminishing language—but it did mean that increasingly our efforts were undermined on Capitol Hill and in the states by those who had professionalized the pro-life movement by their embrace of politicians who could not live with a pure and principled position. While ALL continued to oppose abortion because every abortion kills a fellow human being, many in our ranks increasingly looked at this heinous act as an "issue" to be used to elect less than totally pro-life politicians.

As individuals began considering the race for President, we at ALL, since we could not endorse anyone, found ourselves exam-

Eighteen

ining people on the basis of their ability to articulate defense for all innocent human beings. We never paid attention to their party loyalty. Once again, it seemed, American Life League had drawn a line in the sand and we stood apart from the rest. The claim that we were being divisive arose, and my response was that those who drove a wedge between the children and the political landscape were truly not only the divisive ones, but were creating a chasm into which the bodies of tiny boys and girls were falling at rapidly increasing rates.

As I look back on those preparations for the 1992 elections now, I can see clearly that the basic principle of pro-life unity based on personhood began to unravel as its historically centered approach on the natural law, moral principle and truth began to creep toward a patchwork quilt that was ultimately to break the back of political credibility in the movement within a short span of four years.

Ah! I get ahead of myself, though. What happened between the dawn of the 1992 election season and the actual elections themselves is a tragedy. Vulnerable human beings in the womb did have a champion—Republican contender Patrick J. Buchanan, known for his eloquence, quick wit, and what some would describe as abrasiveness attempting to oppose the party favorite, George Bush.

Pat bowed out of the race early, as did evangelist and television mogul Pat Robertson. But there was a message in Pat Buchanan' campaign that rang true to all of us at American Life League. A man could run for office while at the same time being proud of his faith in God, and his commitment to all preborn children. He might have done poorly in the early days of that race, but he set a standard that would not be denied.

Too many in our movement adopted early the public description of George Bush as pro-life when he was not. Here was a man who had never championed the preborn child, and yet he was touted as "ours." That same year we saw the pro-life finan cial backing and endorsement of candidates like Kay Bailey Hutchinson who ran for and won a Senate seat in Texas. She was considered pro-life only because she said she opposed the Freedom of Choice Act. That meant to the media and the elec torate, that a person who was merely opposed to government involvement in the killing of preborn children could, by virtue of a few words, gain the mantle of pro-life while doing absolutely nothing to advance total protection for all the innocent. Clearly so-called "pro-life politics" had become the art of ignoring truth—a very unwise tactic it seems to me.

Ultimately, America faced a choice between George Bush who was another lip-service-to-the-babies candidate and a little known man from Arkansas, William Jefferson Clinton, who wowed the women, spoke in parables of confusion and ultimately by a plu rality won the White House in 1992. Mr. Clinton and his wife Hillary, had big things in store for the nation, but the nice guy from Arkansas played well with an electorate that was fed up with Washington politicians and really looking for a change.

∽

On the legislative front, during those two years, nothing much happened that was noteworthy, but the Supreme Court dished out a decision in *Planned Parenthood v. Casey* that effectively enshrined abortion and contraception into the Constitution, at least according to the Court; which, as we know, had long ago usurped law-making power from the various state legislatures and deter mined that it was omnipotent in all matters affecting the family and in particular, the vulnerable preborn human being.

The Court made a few ridiculous statements, that I still read with horror. They are these:

"a state may not prohibit any woman from making the ultimate decision to terminate her pregnancy before viability;" and

"the State . . . may . . . regulate, and even proscribe, abortion except where it is necessary, in appropriate medical judgment, for the preservation of the life or health of the mother."

In other words, the U.S. Supreme Court once again, by use of the word "health," in effect sanctioned abortion on demand throughout all nine months of pregnancy.

But perhaps the most chilling phrase from this Supreme Court dictum was, "at the heart of liberty is the right to define one's concept of existence, of meaning, of the universe, of the mystery of life."

The Court recognized the illegitimate power a mother has to define for herself whether or not her child exists and, further, whether or not her child is meaningful. This one statement put the Supreme Court and the culture on a collision course with God and His authority over creation.

∽

On the home front, things were really getting interesting. Christy had overcome her debilitating illness and made the best of it in a most remarkable way by graduating from high school and choosing as her field of professional interest photography. She had a real knack for it and it was clear as 1992 drew to a close that she was destined for great things in the area of artistic impressionism via the lens of large format and normal format cameras. Are those words Greek to you? Well, don't feel bad. Christy's growing interest in photography, development of her own film and strange shoots of subjects in the middle of the night introduced us to many new phrases and techniques we had never heard of before and still don't understand. But she understood and was extremely good at what she had chosen to pursue. She excelled in her field from the first class she decided to take at the local community college.

Hugh completed his college education and, having proposed to his girlfriend Ann in 1991, set the date for their wedding for November 21, 1992. We were duly informed by Ann that this date was chosen simply and only because she was sure that if the anniversary date was the day before his birthday, chances were fairly good that Hugh would not forget it! I, of course, did not have the courage to explain to her that a man can forget his name if his wife doesn't remind him of it—at least that has been my experience!

The wedding was planned with the greatest detail by Ann's parents and even though my dear father was told he could not fly on airplanes because of his weakened heart, he wanted desperately to be at the wedding. To make this dream become a reality he traveled from California to Virginia by train. He looked so handsome in a tuxedo, and there really are no words to describe his joy at being able to be an integral part of his first grandson's wedding, except to say that the look on his face was worth a million dollars! I had seen my dear father in many happy situations but his look on that day was one of the most joyful I can ever remember.

Paul, the man of my dreams, had a surprise up his sleeve, too, for our 25th wedding anniversary, which arrived on December 30, 1992. He had planned an extravaganza. It was an unbelievable

Chester at Hugh's wedding, 1992, his last visit. Left to right: Chester, Christy, Hugh, me, Paul and Cathy

celebration! We had a lovely Mass to renew our vows and a black-tie optional dinner-dance to honor the occasion. It was one of those times in the history of a family that one can only describe as perfect. Everyone was there, including two little people who were not present in the public sense, but rather via womb residence! Hugh and Ann had just conceived our wonderful granddaughter, Emily, and Cathy was six months pregnant with a miracle from God whom she named Anthony.

So, while the pro-life movement was sinking to a new low in some ways, our family was growing spiritually, emotionally and in sheer numbers. The story of one of those tiny human beings, Anthony, deserves a chapter all its own.

Left to Right: Father Denis O'Brien, M.M., Ann Rene Tolson-Brown and Hugh

Mr. and Mrs. Hugh R. Brown
November 21, 1992

God Never Makes a Mistake

1992 AT HOME

Cathy was majoring in marketing at the George Mason University School of Business when she met a young man who stole her heart. He seemed to be a very nice person and we were so pleased to see Cathy happy and committed to someone with whom she had a great deal in common. Their frequent picnics, which were often shared with his daughter from a previous marriage, were a source of great joy for her. In fact, talking with him on the phone made her day. This made Paul and me so happy for her.

One evening in July of 1992 they came to our home as Paul and I were preparing to attend a pro-life dinner in Northern Virginia. When Cathy and her young man arrived I was still getting ready for the evening. Paul greeted them in the family room. Cathy came in to see me, which was a bit unusual, and she proceeded to tell me that she had something important to say.

I looked into her beautiful blue eyes and had an intuitive feeling that escaped from my lips as I said, "You are pregnant aren't you?" She told me that indeed, this was her news, to which I responded with a hug and the comment, "We'll get through this somehow and I do not think you should tell your father." But as

Nineteen

Teach me to do your will, for you are my God. May your good Spirit guide me on level ground.

Psalm 143:10

was telling her this, the baby's father was announcing to Paul that Cathy was pregnant. I recall his comment vividly, because Paul repeated it to me several times during the course of that evening, "I hate to spoil your dinner, but Cathy is pregnant."

Paul reacted in what was perhaps the only way for a father to react in a situation like this one. He asked the young man to leave the house. Cathy and I had emerged from the bedroom by that time and Cathy was surprised to see that her boyfriend was gone, and she was truly upset with her dad when he explained that he had told the young man to leave. Cathy reacted by making statements to her dad about his lack of understanding in this situation and left the house.

At that point it was clear that Paul and I were going to need all the grace and courage we could muster to get through this, not only for Cathy and our first grandchild, but in order to preserve peace in the home and the serenity we felt our daughter would need during the ensuing months. After all, Cathy, her baby and the baby's father were now an integral part of our family, and regardless of how any of us might feel, the fact was that we were welcoming a new human being and that had to be our priority, not only on that evening but for the months ahead.

So we proceeded to go to the dinner. I can tell you now that the situation was a strained one to say the least—it was extremely stressful. I knew that Paul was upset and that the last thing in the world he really wanted to do at that moment was accompany his wife so that she could receive a donation from a local Knights of Columbus Council for American Life League's work. But come he did, and we made it through the event.

The fact is, however, Paul was justifiably outraged by what had occurred. He felt that this young man had taken advantage of Cathy, and he believed that Cathy was an unwilling victim. As a male, he viewed the actions of this young man as those of an aggressor. Paul also felt, initially, that he had the power to convince Cathy that she really had no feelings for this fellow. As it turned out I heard him say many times after this initial reaction that the one thing that occurred to him over and over again was a simple fact of life: "You can't fight love." And, if Cathy truly loved this person, the father of her child, then we were going to have to work through this and step aside. It was not a matter of us treating Cathy like a baby; not at all. Cathy was a mother and she would make the final decision about her relationship with her baby's father. That was a hard and bitter pill for Paul to swallow, but facts are facts.

Still, during the early weeks after our initial conversations with Cathy and her boyfriend, there was a roller coaster of emotions with which we had to deal. Each time that Paul attempted to discuss matters with Cathy, she became justifiably defensive of her position and of the father of her baby, and more than once she turned and left the house. As I look back on this now, I can see that we made some critical errors in judgment. It appears now that at least some of our response was based on our own interpretation of someone else's feelings. In this case, that someone else was our daughter—a very level-headed young woman who had already decided that she and her baby were going to overcome whatever obstacles might get in their way in order to be joyful in new life and happy with the coming months and years of her motherhood. She exhibited tremendous willpower; I did not even realize how much until it came time for me to write this chapter.

What do I mean? When two parents have a child who is as

much of a blessing to them as Cathy is to us, it is very easy for remarks, comments and judgments to fly way off the mark. While Paul and I might have thought that certain steps should be taken by Cathy, we kept forgetting that this was Cathy's life and decisions were going to be made by her in the light of her own feelings, her own faith and her own strategy. Cathy put up with far more from Paul and me than these few pages can relate, but eventually we all got on the same wavelength, thank God.

Let's look at a few of those experiences. After much conversing, screaming, door slamming and leaving, Cathy came to a point of peace with her father. She and her boyfriend decided to meet with the pastor of our church and discuss the entire situation, including their hopes to be married in the Catholic Church. After the first of these meetings, our pastor decided that he really liked the young man and that he would work with both of them so that they could properly prepare for a wedding.

We had a lovely dinner in our home shortly after that first meeting and everything seemed to be going along very well. Cathy and I spent one day shopping for a wedding gown for her and bridesmaid dresses for her sister and three of her friends. We were so happy to find a beautiful gown, one that looked smashing on Cathy, a princess without the gown, after all.

The meetings with our pastor continued, and after a time it was clear that things were not going along as well as we had hoped. There seemed to be a few doubts coming forth from the pastor's discussion with the baby's father, and Cathy's own instincts were becoming less than positive. What we had hoped would be a smooth seven months was becoming a bit rocky, and we faced a whole new set of circumstances that no one could have foretold. Our pastor was concerned that Cathy's boyfriend was not totally committed to her and the baby. He was concerned that perhaps a wedding planned in haste could produce negative consequences for everyone concerned and recommended that a great deal more time be taken prior to anyone deciding whether or not marriage was the proper solution. I think, in retrospect, that he knew a great deal more about the chemistry between Cathy and this fellow that he ever discussed with us, but I also know that infatuation is not the same as love. While I would have hoped that the seeds of true love would grow between the two of them, I knew that this meant that both of them would have to sacrifice a great deal and it was not clear that Cathy's boyfriend was willing to give to the extent that she was already giving. This is why we became concerned once again.

Cathy was becoming increasingly worried about whether or not the young man really loved her enough to be there for her and the baby. The depth of her concerns was such that she agreed to discuss the possibility of getting this fellow to sign an agreement that would involve him with the baby but first involve him in the financial support required for both her and the baby. A document was drawn up by the family attorney and shipped off to the young man. We all waited for a response. As it turned out, he did not want to agree to provide financial support for the baby. I honestly believe that at that point in time Cathy had lost all hope that this young man ever loved her. Cathy had dreamed of a family unit that would be together forever and would increasingly love one another and other children who might come along later. She did not believe that this scenario was possible with this particular young man at the time.

Paul and I were relieved. You can call it a sixth sense; you can call it intuition; you can call it any number of things. In my heart of hearts I wanted to believe that Cathy's love for this fellow

Paul with
Cathy during
her pregnancy.

would be strong enough to carry the rocky start to the next plateau—a firm foundation based on mutual love and self-sacrifice—but I couldn't. Accepting responsibility for a baby, a wife, and all that goes along with a marriage was not something I felt this young man was up to at the moment. And the fact that he affirmed that fear of mine by his reaction to the document hurt me, but it truly devastated Cathy.

In late August, after this sad experience, I asked Cathy if she would like to fly to Los Angeles with Christy and me to visit my father. Paul and I thought it would be good for Cathy, giving her some new scenery for a while and the opportunity to see her grandfather. She was hesitant about what her grandfather might say to her about the baby, but we discussed this and we all decided that the trip should be made.

We had been at Daddy's house for a couple of days when Cathy finally decided that the time was right and she had this unforgettable conversation with my Dad:

"Grandpa, I am pregnant and I suppose you will hate me for it."

In his usual way, he replied to her,

"Cathy, how could you say that? I love you, I am proud of you and there is nothing you could ever do that would make me hate you, especially not having a baby!"

Cathy's face glowed and I silently thanked God for this moment, which after all of the previous moments we had lived through over the past couple of months, was a joyous one. Yes, Daddy spoke to Cathy about what she should not have done, how her life would change forever with the birth of the baby; but he never, ever made her feel cheap or bad or wrong. He cushioned every word he said to her with loving kindness. After all, that was my Dad!

After that trip, the celebration began. We had baby furniture to purchase, showers to plan for Cathy and her son, and that wonderful move. Cathy had requested that she be able to live at home, so we moved her out of her apartment and into our home. We arranged Hugh's room (he was married by this time) as a nursery and we did all that we could to make Cathy feel at ease. She was wonderful, of course, and experienced a totally problem-free pregnancy. She continued to attend school at George Mason University until December of 1992 and then took a 9-month leave so she could prepare for the baby and be home with him for the first three months of his life. She had always planned to be married and to be able to stay home and raise a very large family while her husband cared for her and the children, so adjusting to the role of single mother could have devastated her. It did not.

As I have had to reflect on this situation, and sought Cathy's assistance with this particular chapter of my life as her mother, it causes me some sorrow to know that there are people who, for whatever reason, have not been blessed with the strength necessary to carry on when difficulty emerges. The young man who is the father of our amazing grandson needs our prayers, and he needs our sacrifices too. God works in very strange ways sometimes, and one must believe in miracles. I do!

When I first sat down to write about this particular experience in my life with my family, it was my daughter who reminded me about the simple fact that no one must ever judge the intention or the action of another. That is a job that only God can do.

She has also reminded me, by her own extremely competent handling of the situation despite her sorrow, her broken heart and her sacrifice, that living in a state of trusting God completely requires a human being to surrender himself fully to God and never look back. Whether or not a healing occurs in the relationship our grandson's father has with his son and the mother of his child is God's domain, never ours. What we can do is hope and pray that in His time all things will work for the good of these three human beings who are integrally related to each other not only through the wonder of procreating a child in the image and likeness of God, but in God's only-begotten Son. Each of us can seek forgiveness for our transgressions before Him and experience His mercy within the depths of our souls. That is my prayer for this young man. It is never too late to heal that which has been broken.

May God guide our grandson's father in His spirit on level ground!

Chapter

Good bye, Daddy! 1993

The year got off to a very exciting start for us. Paul and I spent an anniversary of absolute wonder traveling to Brazil and spent two weeks enjoying each other while things at home settled down for a while, at least. When we returned, we had more preparations to make for the new grandchild who would be welcomed into our home. We had the moods of our dear one, Cathy, to balance against the interests of Christy, who was trying desperately to complete her credits at the local community college so that she could go on to New York University's Tisch School of the Arts. You might say those first three months of 1993 were a bit harried! I think it is fair to say that as the mother hen I spent much more time at home, which is where I belonged, than I did anywhere else.

Around 9 p.m. on March 16, Cathy assured us all that she was in labor. Since I had been her coach during the Lamaze classes, she and I drove to the hospital, having been instructed by Grandpa Paul and Christy to call when things looked like they might actually start happening. And, happen they did. At about 9 a.m. on St. Patrick's day, March 17, Cathy gave birth to Anthony Sean Brown, a six-pound bundle of joy! She chose "Anthony" because her dad's middle name is Anthony, and she chose

Twenty

In him who is the source of my strength, I have strength for everything.

Phil. 4:13

"Sean" for—well—the Irish!

Christy took all the photos one would want to have of a birth, and a video, too. She was even salesman enough to convince Cathy's obstetrician that she should be allowed to follow Anthony into the nursery and record for posterity the scrubbing, the wrapping and the laying of the newborn child in the bassinet in the nursery where he would be observed for a short time before he returned to his mother's waiting arms.

Grandfather attended, of course, but chose not to witness the actual arrival of his grandson, preferring to visit with mother and child an hour later. I can't say that I blame him really; once around that block with his own children had clearly been sufficient.

∽

We adjusted the household, and I took a two-week leave of absence in order to wait on Cathy and take care of all her daily needs so that she could give full time to her son. All progressed beautifully for both of them and our home was, as it had been 20 years earlier, a place of constant running, diapering and tending. It was so much fun!

In June, however, my dear father became very ill, and Paul and I flew out to Los Angeles to be with him. He had been taken to the emergency room of a local hospital and, unable to speak, he had written on a pad of paper that he wished to have a tracheotomy tube placed in his lungs to help him breathe. No one in that emergency room was paying any attention to his requests at all! Thank God we were there to inform them, by showing them his note, that he did not wish to die of suffocation.

It made me wonder how many patients like him, who have no loved ones standing by, do die because no one is paying attention or, even worse, because someone has consciously decided that this particular person is about to die anyway, so why bother?

Daddy made progress, and he came home from the hospital, and we went back home leaving him in the able hands of his wonderful sister, Mildred, who lived with him. Then, in late July we got another call. He was seriously ill again and no one really expected him to leave the hospital, so I flew out there alone to be with him. Again, he fooled them all and came home on a Friday. I left that Sunday to go back to my home, assuring my aunt that she should go ahead and leave town and spend some time with her children. She really did not want to leave Daddy, but I told her that he would let me know if anything went wrong or if he needed me. Fortunately she did not listen to me.

I was home one day, and the call came that he had been

Cathy and Anthony.

Me holding Emily.

taken to the hospital again and was in ICU. I flew out that time with Christy, who really should have been preparing to leave for New York but who wanted to be with her favorite person, her grandfather. On August 10 he died. Daddy's heart had simply given up after so many battles fought so valiantly. He never got out of ICU but he knew who was with him until about 48 hours before his death. Cathy and Anthony arrived two days before his death, but because of the possibility of infectious disease, Anthony never met his grandfather in person, though he did meet him from the womb and certainly had won his heart even then.

Daddy died in peace and without pain, for he had a respirator to assist his breathing right up until the end. He had also spoken with a priest, and though I cannot be certain that he was received into the Catholic Church days before his death, I somehow have the feeling that he was. It just seems right, after all, considering his life of giving, loving and caring—especially for my mother. He was always the wonderful husband, the caring father, the doting grandfather. He was a simple man who had a huge heart and a remarkable commitment to live what he believed rather than talk about it.

∞

I remember reading a letter my son Hugh wrote. Hugh could not be at the funeral because Ann was due to have Emily any time, but he did write a great tribute to his grandfather, and in those few words expressed a love for someone dear, sweet and kind. I will miss my dad just as much as I miss my mother, but all too often since then I have realized that, though they are not here in a physical sense, both of them are here and still taking good care of me, even when I really need a good swift kick where it will do the most good, if you know what I mean.

∞

September 29 brought Emily face to face with the world, and where Daddy had been there were now two precious children to carry on the tradition of family love that grows in adversity, flowers in times of trial and beckons to one and all to come in and relax while we meditate on how terrific it is just to have each other.

Chapter

Religious Right?

I could have called this chapter, "Here we go again" but decided against doing so out of respect for Ronald Reagan, who at least admitted that he was often wrong and off track on matters of principle! I can't say that for some people in positions of presumed leadership in the pro-life political movement. But I don't want to write here about people, I want to use this chapter to share with you the difference between false righteousness and true adherence to the Lord's command that we be the servants of all if we wish to follow Him into eternity.

∽

Back in 1993 after William Jefferson Clinton took office, he promised to rid the country of as many preborn children as possible. Oh yes he did! Well, you might respond, he never said that. Oh, but his actions spoke louder than all the words he ever spoke from that date forward.

Remember on January 22, the memorial anniversary of *Roe v. Wade/Doe v. Bolton*, when he, by executive order, lifted the ban on human embryo research, struck down the Reagan language that prohibited the U.S. from being involved in anti-life population control programs, eradicated the abortion-counseling prohibition (so-

Twenty-one

called "gag" rule) from federally funded programs, and swiftly sent the Department of Justice scurrying after ways to put as many pro-lifers as possible in jail? That tactic, better known as the Freedom of Access to Clinic Entrances Act (FACE), came about within days of his dastardly executive orders and sent shivers down everyone's spine. When he wasn't looking at jailing many of us, he was examining ways to embrace the culture of death in a new health care policy—remember?

In 1994 the FACE Act passed Congress with little more than a whimper from our friends on Capitol Hill, and ALL had to fight it in court. It occurred to me then, when the bill passed, that our fair-weather allies in Congress were really not interested in protecting those who speak up for the preborn child, let alone protecting the preborn child. They were somehow intimidated by the frantic and over-zealous rhetoric of the pro-abortion cabal, including the Attorney General, Janet Reno, who made sweeping derogatory statements against pro-life activists with no basis in fact. ALL felt abandoned by its colleagues on the so-called religious right who apparently were saving their efforts for some greater battle than that of protecting the men and women who placed their very selves in harm's way for that one brief opportunity they might have to reach out in love and convince a mother that there really are people in this world who would love and accept her and her innocent baby if only she would choose life.

ALL sued Janet Reno, and though we lost at the federal appeals level when the Supreme Court refused to grant us certiori (a hearing of the arguments), I believe we gave courage to others in the pro-life activist movement so that again and again that law was challenged in court and, as I complete this updated version of my autobiography, the jury is still out on this draconian law. There are so many challenges to this unjust law coming through the court system now, because of our pioneering effort, that sooner or later we may yet see the law overturned. It is a law, by the way, that in my view can effectively be used to silence and jail even those who silently pray in front of abortion mills or peacefully picket in front of the homes of those who earn their living killing the innocent.

ﾟﾟﾟﾟﾟﾟﾟﾟﾟﾟﾟﾟﾟﾟﾟﾟﾟﾟﾟﾟﾟﾟﾟﾟﾟﾟﾟ∽

During this same year there were races for Congressional seats once again. And the thing that really began to bother me in those early months of 1994 was the reduction that was made in pro-life currency—devaluation of principle.

I believe that if God were instructing His disciples today in the art of political strategy and how to go about protecting the weak and the vulnerable among them, He would expect them to hold up a standard of exactly the same type as He preached during his time on earth. This standard would be based on His admonition that if man refuses to acknowledge Him here on earth, He will not acknowledge man before His Father, God. In the case of abortion, He would expect His disciples to teach and preach the Commandments and the Beatitudes. What better political strategy could anyone want, after all?

No, the message would probably not present a standard that everyone applauded, because it would mean that the same kind of action taken by the disciples would have to be taken by everyone, unselfishly and without ever considering the personal cost to income, reputation or popularity. It might even mean that at the end of the election cycle a disciple's position in defense of all innocent human beings would result in defeat at the polls. Nonetheless, it would be a standard that man, in his sinfulness, could strive toward with the single desire of pleasing God as his motivation and his inspiration. Some might think that my proposal is seriously flawed because it doesn't take into consideration the political realities of the 90s, and I would suggest that this is precisely why we should embrace the strategy. How do you promote conversion if you have no sound platform on which to stand and teach?

∞

Well, back to currency. To be labeled pro-life in the 1994 Congressional races meant that you could oppose one particular type of regulatory abortion reform, or at the most, government spending on abortion. It also meant that you could hold these positions and say, publicly and without explanation or apology, that your position must include exceptions for rape, incest, and the life of the mother. If you happened to measure up to these drastically reduced standards, you could expect to receive endorsements, and some sort of publicity from the National Right to Life Committee, Christian Coalition activists who were involved personally in political battles, and many (if not all) so called "right-wing" or "religious right" groups.

To the average political candidate in 1994, being pro-life meant doing as little as you could, as infrequently as you could, and as quietly as you could for preborn children. It meant that nearly anyone who opposed even 1/100th of all abortions done in the U.S. could wear the pro-life label and get publicity in church bulletins and elsewhere—running around the district or the state saying "I am pro-life," while laughing up his sleeve. It meant that the American people who really trusted pro-life leaders to tell them who was and who wasn't pro-life, were being misled, misguided—deceived. On purpose? You bet!

∞

Why? Because too many strategists and tacticians within the movement had reached a point in their area of expertise where winning a majority for the Republican party was the most important goal of all.

Am I not being judgmental here—just a bit? No, I don't

think so. Remember, when the pro-life movement started, our goal was to restore total protection to all preborn children by passing either a constitutional amendment that restored legal personhood to every innocent human being from fertilization to death, or a law requiring a simple majority that would accomplish the same thing. Why? Because we knew back in the early 70s that every single abortion killed one of our brothers or our sisters, and we were intolerant of this illicit and gravely immoral act. But by the mid-90s that vision had been altered by pragmatism, relativism and perceived political power. The 30-second sound bite became more relevant than the words of truth that would have touched a nerve in American politics that many of our allies were unwilling to touch.

In other words, somewhere along the way the religious right had taken a wrong turn.

Immediately after those elections, if you recall, we were told that the American people had elected the most pro-life Congress in the history of the movement. Sadly, far too many people believed that and went along with the language of the day. In the process the pro-life label—and what it meant in politics— nearly became extinct as a measure of moral fortitude, or what I would call integrity.

∽

In our family, everyone was doing just fine. Emily and Anthony had become fast friends, walking, talking a language of

Emily and
Anthony.

their own, and charming everyone. How do I know this? Because when you are sitting at Mass with a small child who just can't keep his or her tongue and movements in check, reactions could go one of two ways. Smiles always appeared on even the most stern of faces.

My personal life was filled with the joys of being a grandma—what a wonderful experience! I had always thought that motherhood was fantastic, but this was beyond compare. Where else can you divest yourself of all decorum to roll around on a floor, sound like an animal, and act like a complete and total nut? Only grandmas and grandpas are allowed to do that sort of thing and still be accepted as adults!

Chapter

Celebrate The Gospel of Life 1995

On March 25, 1995, Pope John Paul II issued the extraordinary encyclical *The Gospel of Life*. This 180-page document has been described as a "love letter" to all people of good will, and once I had read this document I agreed. Truly in the pages of this Biblically based message one finds the reasons behind the culture of death, the positive signs in our own culture for hope and renewal and, most important, the inspiration to live the Gospel of life every day of one's life.

The average person reading this now is probably thinking, "What is this woman talking about? How can a message on moral principle and God's Word apply to me in my life? She's really lost it now!"

No, wait a minute. I think that every single person, called as each of us is by God to a work known only in our heart, really needs to be affirmed, uplifted and validated in our daily life. We look at the ordinary things that we do every day and really can't see how they mesh with the big picture—saving souls and bringing our fellow human beings into a conversation with God. But the truth is that the simplest act of kindness can bring about amazing changes in the entire world! How? Christ walked the earth and touched the lives of average people like you and me one by one. He brought the

Twenty-two

"All scripture is inspired of God and is useful for teaching—for reproof, correction, and training in holiness so that the man of God may be fully competent and equipped for every good work."

2 Tim. 3:16–17

good news to them by preaching, loving and healing. We too are blessed with the ability to do this each time we pat a person on the back, hug a child, go out of our way to do a good deed for a loved one, change a diaper, mop a floor, or help someone who is clearly at wits-end with the overflowing grocery cart or stack of files in the office. By being servants of life we are affirming God's love in our actions and our words. This is important because every pro-life good deed is a part of the plan our Father has for all mankind in ways we cannot even begin to comprehend. That's why we are the workers and He is the boss!

In other words, what *The Gospel of Life* recalls for each of us is that in our daily lives there are countless opportunities to thank God for loving us and for caring enough to breathe life into us; and to show our gratitude by the way we treat others. No matter what it is that we do, if we do it out of love and gratitude to Him, it counts in His work of restoring our culture by using us as His hands and His feet.

In retrospect I can now tell you that what happened at ALL after this encyclical was published was truly of God. I became totally motivated to make the messages of this encyclical come alive for all those who work in defense of life and the larger numbers of people who truly are living the pro-life message but are probably unaware of it. I sat down with the members of our staff, and we decided that it would be very helpful if ALL created a series of personal and group study guides on this encyclical, books that would help others grasp the inspiring words of this document, apply those words to their own lives, and create the desire to spread those words to others, or just absorb them into one's thoughts.

Further, it occurred to me that the very best thing we could do to offset the confusion in some areas of pro-life leadership was to provide our fellow Americans with as much of God's truth as we could in a format that was easily understood and adaptable on a personal level.

For me at least, the message of this encyclical embodied all that was necessary for men and women of good will to set about the task of renewing our community and spreading the joy that was at the very basis of everything that we did to end the killing of innocent human beings. After all, one can either curse the darkness or one can light a candle, as the saying goes, and this particular document prepared by Pope John Paul II is a collection of the most brilliant, awesome points of light I had ever read in my life.

I can also look back on my experiences and see that there is total affirmation in that document for the controversial positions ALL had taken over the years in that it was clear, once again, that every innocent human being is an expression of God's love for the world. Man is, after all, His reflection, and to harm even one of these, our brothers and sisters, is to join with Cain and ask God: "Am I my brother's keeper?" The answer to this question (which is still asked today) is: "Yes you are."

We as pro-life people, above all others, must always respond, "Yes!" So the work began. We worked very hard on our draft copies of four different study guides for *The Gospel of Life* and one on the 1993 encyclical *The Splendor of Truth*. Many have suggested that *The Splendor of Truth* really is the backdrop for *The Gospel of Life,* and we agree. One concentrates on how man's conscience is properly formed, while the other takes man and his conscience through the wonder and miraculous nature of God's gift of life and Satan's efforts to destroy it.

So, can you imagine how exciting it was for me, and other select members of our staff, to attend a special meeting in the Vatican on the topic of *The Gospel of Life*? Can you identify with the thrill I had at being able to hand a draft copy of our study guides directly to Pope John Paul II, ask for his blessing on our work and on you, and stand in his presence as he smiled and encouraged my husband and me? It was an experience that is really difficult for me to describe, short of saying thank you to God for calling me to this work and somehow keeping me sane enough to do it with faith and, I hope, appreciation of His love for me and those I love.

By the end of 1995 ALL had completed this set of books, a truly enormous task, that provided the blueprint any one could use to live, breathe and proclaim the Gospel of life!

It is also evident that this renewal was needed for me because of what I saw going on around me in the movement. There was a sense in far too many places that our job was not ending the killing through social and political tactics, but rather regulating it to the best of our ability. There appeared to be a sense of resignation

Me with Pope John Paul II.

to the evil, and I prayed very hard that through our humble efforts we could, at least to a small degree, renew enthusiasm for life as the basis for all that was proposed and pursued in the coming years. It was clear to me then, as it is today, that the antidote to compromise is the unequivocal commitment to the Gospel of life. If each one of us is in solidarity with every other human being, then it is easy to stand up and proclaim the truth and never count the cost.

∽

This glorious year also brought our third grandchild, Kaitlynn Irene, who was conceived in September and announced to us on Thanksgiving eve by proud parents Hugh and Ann. Emily would now have a little sister, and from the very minute they learned of the arrival of their second child, Hugh and Ann involved Emily in the preparations to welcome her sister into the world.

Christy, now in her final year at New York University, fell in love, and her intended went through the formality of coming to our home and asking Paul for her hand in marriage. His name is Thomas, and from the first moment I met him it was clear that God had found the perfect soul mate for our creative daughter. She is, after all, an artist, and her way of living would be described by many as a bit unusual, but her very being always exuded enthusiasm and true love for life. Thomas identified with that at once and appreciated her for who she is, so we found him

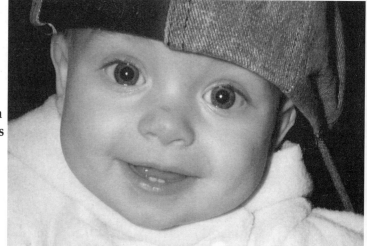

Kaitlynn
8 months
old.

to be a wonderful choice and a second son who would fit right in to our family with ease.

Cathy got her degree, another sign of her remarkable fortitude, and moved on to the task of raising Anthony and holding down a job that would provide for them and give her the self-reliance and independence she needed in order to make her way in the world.

Clearly, for me, these three children of ours exemplified the bottom line of *The Gospel of Life*—appreciation of the various gifts God gives to each of us and our own personal struggles to identify those gifts, improve on them through faith and good works and celebrate them by nurturing those around us who deserve our love and kindness even when we are tempted to do otherwise. I am a one-man fan club for my children, I know, but of all the remarkable things God has done in my life, all the struggles He has assigned to me and all the many things that He has accomplished as I stand back in awe of His majesty, the most truly wondrous gifts He has bestowed on me are my husband and children.

The grandchildren are, to put it in words, a bonus and a tribute to His glory, His gift of procreation, and His everlasting love for all mankind. Every time I play with one of them or even think about them I remember that in them is His promise that He loves man more than man could know and will truly be with each us always and in every way until the end of time.

Cathy receives her diploma.

Chapter

Infanticide and Unity
1996

When I first began volunteering in the pro-life movement in 1969, I never thought that a day would come when I would have to sit down and tell anyone how a weakened movement arrived at a juncture where many of its chief spokesmen and strategists were leading a fight to regulate one specific type of child-killing by first redefining it and then proceeding to legislate against it with a life-of-the-mother exception. But that is exactly what happened the day the partial-birth abortion ban came on the horizon.

What is a so-called "partial-birth" abortion?

When this deadly procedure is carried out, the process is begun by using chemicals to prematurely begin the birth process. The chemicals dilate the cervix. When the mother's cervix is sufficiently dilated (this usually takes two days), instruments are used to deliver nearly all of the preborn baby, first his legs, then his torso and finally his arms so that all that remains within the mother is the child's head. At that point, a specific type of scissors is used to puncture the back of the child's head so that his brains can be sucked out and his head collapsed, thus making it possible to complete the delivery of a now-dead human being.

This is actually infanticide, for the child is not dead until

Twenty-three

"But the wise shall shine brightly like the splendor of the firmament, and those who lead the many to justice shall be like the stars forever.

Dan. 12:3

seconds before delivery is complete.

Why, then, call it abortion? It doesn't make any sense. A baby is delivered except for his head, and then that baby is killed.

Yes, it is horrific; and yes, it is murder, but one has to ask why the pro-life movement would have, in large part, focused its attention on this act of infanticide specifically and exclusively during an election year or, for that matter, at any time.

Is there now such a thing as a bad abortion? Could it be that the millions done each year by chemical, device and instrument are somehow less urgent to oppose than this act of infanticide? Or is it ultimately that many political strategists in our ranks decided that it was futile to work for the total protection of all innocent human beings from fertilization? I cannot say exactly, for I do not wish to impugn the motives of any one or any organization's thinkers, but clearly, something awful happened to many of the political strategists in this movement, and subsequently to the electorate in 1996.

Remember the facts. An innocent human being's life begins at fertilization and continues, if not interrupted by a birth control pill, emergency contraception (mega-doses of the pill), an IUD, Depo-Provera, Norplant, RU-486, methotrexate, or surgical act, until birth begins. There are many children lost naturally through miscarriage, which is a sad and debilitating event for the parents, but the children lost by any of these other means are killed on purpose. There are millions of them who die each year, and only God knows how many Mother Teresas, Jim Dobsons and other heroic figures have met their death by abortion.

This is why the pro-life movement started—to help others see the value of a human being at every stage of his or her life, to be the moral conscience for a nation somehow deliberately in denial over the reality of these deaths, to sound a clarion call to everyone and anyone in a perceived position of power, demanding an end to the state-sanctioned destruction of our own brothers and sisters. This is why we formed organizations in our communities, our states and our nation's capital—isn't it?

In 1996 we forgot our roots. We forgot that opinion polls do not dictate moral principle nor do they in any way modify the natural law. We forgot that elected officials are called to serve all of the human beings in their constituency, including those whose lives have just begun. We forgot that the goal of ending all abortion means never succumbing to political pressure but always rising above it because of the Father whom we serve and for whom the death of each of His children is a tragedy beyond description. We forgot that statistics and political compromise have absolutely nothing to do with the wages of such massive human destruction that will be exacted from a nation that is virtually desensitized by the human carnage—a body count that rises every few seconds of every single day.

We forgot our faith. For too many of us, our own personal wisdom became more of a guidepost than the wisdom with which we are endowed if we surrender ourselves to the Author of life. And so it was that we focused our attention on a clear act of infanticide, redefined it as abortion (4/5 infanticide, 1/5 abortion, as one brochure claimed) and then proceeded in 1996, another election year, to defend as pro-life those politicians who opposed this specific act of killing regardless of where he or she stood on any other kind.

Yes, President Clinton vetoed this bill, and no, the Congress could not muster the votes, in the Senate that is, to override the veto; but does that teach us something about the moral decay of the political scene, or does it teach us something about ourselves? Is the lesson that perhaps we, as pro-life Americans, have expected too little and given away too much?

∽

I ask these very tough questions for some very good reasons. The following also happened in 1996:

• The Food and Drug Administration, under Clinton, held hearings on the use of mega-dose birth control pills—called emergency contraception—and found no reason to oppose such use. Did you know they did this even though not one pharmaceutical company asked for these hearings but only the pro-abortion cartel? And did you know that not one study exists to show how dangerous such use could be to the mother, and the deadly effect it has on preborn babies?

• The Planned Parenthood Federation of America began discussing, publicly and with boldness, the use of RU-486 within its clinics after the Food and Drug Administration, under Clinton, held hearings on the abortion drug and suggested that it was within months of approving it.

• Did you know that the cancer treatment methotrexate, a highly toxic drug, when added to misoprostol, can be used to kill preborn babies during their first few weeks of life and that hardly any organization in the pro-life movement worked against this except ALL and Pharmacists for Life?

• Did you know that during 1996 a tremendous movement was under way among those who promote *in vitro* fertilization to use quality control standards so that only acceptable human embryos (tiny human beings) would be considered for implantation in the mother's womb?

Each of these methods was widely touted in the press nearly all year long, but nary a whimper came from the vast majority of pro-life groups as they concentrated all their funding, their efforts and their constituencies on the so-called partial-birth abortion ban—which contained a life of the mother exception.

And do you remember that every single innocent human being is a manifestation of God's love for all mankind, a whisper of that love for each and every other human being to hear, to welcome and to celebrate?

Yes, something is terribly wrong with the political pro-life movement. And the remedy is unity, but of a specific variety.

It is not the kind of unity that can be had by sitting around the conference table and trying to find common ground by avenues that lead to compromise. We do not have that right, because we are talking about the fate of a human being and for us, at least in theory, not even one of them is expendable.

It is not the kind of unity expressed by Ronald Reagan's 11th commandment—never speak ill of your fellow Republicans (or in this case, pro-lifer). No, we are called by God to speak to our brother when we feel that he is doing something wrong, and if he does not heed us we are called to expose that wrong to all those who will hear and comprehend it.

It is the kind of unity that is expressed, lived and advocated in the reality of our own powerlessness, our own human frailty, our own absolute need to rely wholly on God and not ever on ourselves.

If the 1996 elections did not prove to us that a little bit of abortion opposition is deadly to the credibility and the real goals of our work, nothing ever will. We enter the period of the 105th Congress with the weakness of a man standing on one leg and ready to collapse if not given immediate assistance. We enter this period with a challenge, with a hope and with a prayer.

We are focused now, I hope, on renewal of a spiritual kind, and in that reflection ALL will remain steadfastly committed to the

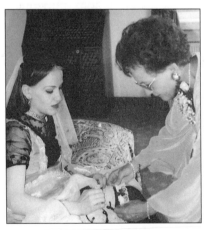

Me with Christy the morning of the wedding.

Paul skipping with Christy.

principles of faith first, action second and total reliance on God as a foundation. We call on others to do likewise but will no longer await their response. There are children dying every day, and while it is true that we are called to minister to those in need and be servants to all, it is equally true that we are never called to abide sin—and abortion is the worst sin of all, in my view.

∽

A few final notes about 1996 that have absolutely nothing to do with death, destruction and evil prowling the world and tempting man in his weakness.

Christy and Thomas got married on July 11 in Ireland. Yes, we now have Thomas as a full fledged member of the Brown clan, and we are ecstatic. He is a gifted musician, a real talent but what makes us so pleased to welcome him is that he is truly in love with our daughter.

We also have Kaitlynn Irene with us in the flesh, and she is as wonderful as her big sister, Emily. Hugh and Ann are remarkable parents and it shows. And, yes, Cathy and Anthony moved into their own home in October of this year—and on we go with the life of the family. Praise God!

Celebrate your loved ones today, won't you? The good news is that each and every one of us is a blessing, and blessings should be shared, appreciated and hugged.

Christy and Tom.

Anthony, the Leprachaun ring bearer and cousin Ellen.

Chapter

The Future Is Ours

The history of the pro-life movement—your history and mine—continues to be written. As we look to the future, there are some difficult realities with which we must deal. It is better to do this sooner than later, so that we can be mentally and spiritually prepared for the challenges that lie ahead.

First let's take a look at the Supreme Court. Some recent decisions may help us see which way the court is headed.

Many pro-lifers did not notice the court's decision in the Johnson Controls case. In this case, the court ruled that a company may not take special precautions to protect its female employees from hazardous chemicals, since to do so would be to discriminate against them on the basis of sex. This was specifically applied even to women who are pregnant or who may desire to become pregnant in the future.

The court decided this case unanimously, which means that not even one justice looked beyond the feminist agenda to consider the possibility that the life of a preborn child might be worth protecting. The court considered only the career aspirations of the mother. No thought whatever was given to the rights of the preborn

Twenty-four

What I tell you in the dark, speak in the daylight; what is whispered in your ear, proclaim from the roofs.

Matt. 10:27

baby. Once again, the court simply refused to acknowledge the personhood of the preborn child.

As vacancies on the court have arisen in recent years, much speculation has focused on whether enough votes will ever exist to overturn *Roe v. Wade*. Naturally, I hope this vicious ruling will be overturned, and the sooner the better, but when one considers rulings like that in *Planned Parenthood v. Casey* in 1992, common sense dictates that we look elsewhere for a solution. After all, overturning *Roe* will not, in itself, put an end to the killing. It will only send the question back to the states, where it was before. As long as the justices refuse even to address the fundamental issue of personhood, no meaningful protection of the preborn is going to come from the Supreme Court.

What about Congress? As I write these words, there are fewer reliable pro-life votes in the House and Senate than at any time since the early 1980s. For a thoroughly pro-life bill, one providing genuine protection for babies in the womb, to even be considered we must first have a unified leadership in this movement willing to demand such a bill—please, God, allow that to happen soon!

What about the state legislatures? In 1995, many regulatory bills were proposed and discussed. A few passed, but court challenges abound. And of these, not one would provide a suitable test case for the Supreme Court to consider the issue of personhood.

The media, of course, continue to mislead the public with solidly pro-abortion rhetoric. In 1991 the Supreme Court actually handed down a pro-life decision, holding in *Rust v. Sullivan* that government had a right to say whether tax dollars could be used to pay for the promotion and referral of abortion. The pro-abortion forces claimed that this ruling "gagged" them. It did no such thing, of course. They were still free to promote killing all they want. They just can't use your tax dollars—or mine—to do it. But the media focused exclusively on the so-called "gag" effect at the time, and Clinton has now dismissed it by using the powers of the presidency to require states to actually pay for many abortions, commensurate with his philosophy.

Seems like a pretty grim picture, doesn't it? Well, there's only one thing to do—redouble our efforts to turn things around! Worrying about past failures won't help. Crying over missed opportunities won't help. Whining about lack of resources and volunteers won't help. We need to start changing the situation. Right now. Right where we are. Today.

What should you do? Why not let the Lord tell you? Pray sincerely and ask Him how He wants to use you. I do not know what the Lord wants of you. But I do know that you can find out if you ask Him. Perhaps our greatest need as a movement is for more prayer, more fasting, more earnest seeking of God's perfect will.

∽

Let me tell you what American Life League is doing to carry on its tradition of leadership in the pro-life arena. We remain, as always, committed to protecting all preborn children, as well their mothers and fathers, and all those whose right to life is threatened.

First, we are committed to countering the extraordinary media bias that essentially denies pro-life people a forum for their views equal to those who espouse the pro-death ethic. Since we cannot depend on the media to tell our story accurately and fairly, we placed a television studio in our office so that, at a moment's notice, when news is breaking, all a network or local station need do is call us and within minutes we are available by satellite to provide a reasoned pro-life response to any question that arises.

This concept of total media savvy at ALL is catching on slowly with the networks, but over time it will be a tremendous asset to the babies.

In addition, *Celebrate Life!* videos are available for airing on any local cable access station. The 76 programs are valuable teaching tools in any situation where pictures can tell a story better than words. These 22-minute videos, designed for television, focus on ordinary people doing extraordinary things, constantly bringing new faces into the spotlight. As a matter of fact, many of these videos have been used effectively to save lives, teach the value of chastity to young people and bring faces and human experiences to the burning questions of euthanasia and physician-assisted suicide as well as neonatal care and abortion.

෴

You may be asking, what about my neighbor, my classmate, my co-worker? How can I prepare myself to share the pro-life message with him or her?

Here are some tools ALL can put into your hands:

Celebrate Life, American Life League's acclaimed magazine, is filled with educational reports, true stories, and access to other resources that can help you, your family, and your group make a difference for the babies. It gives you confidence in discussing difficult topics and late-breaking events, knowing that what you have to say is reliable and accurate.

communiqué, a handy, four-page newsletter that comes out every two weeks. I put a lot of time into this publication, which focuses on short, concise reports on life-related developments in medicine, social policy, politics, and the activities of pro-death organizations coast to coast. If you need a quick, easy-to-use resource for timely news, action items, and resource referrals, write to me and ask to receive *communiqué.*

Resource Catalog, our listing of every publication and video produced or promoted by American Life League. If you have a particular question or concern, I guarantee you will find at least one item in this listing that will help you articulate the problem and give a credible solution in easy-to-understand language.

LIFE LIBRARIES are put together in our office by a team of experts from around the nation. Each library is designed

Throughout the past 24 years, our family has grown in spirituality, maturity, and dedication to the preborn, their mothers and their fathers. We love each other very much, and here we are in January 1992, enjoying precious time together— the five Browns: Paul, Judie, Hugh, Cathy and Christy.

to serve a unique purpose when placed in a community center where people congregate. For example, we have life libraries for schools, doctors' offices, churches and parents. What a terrific way to have ready access to the teaching tools we all need to share with others as we convert America into a culture of life!

LIFE GUIDES are a series of small books on the difficult questions facing us today as we battle the culture of death. Each has been carefully written, and they are designed to help educate our fellow Americans. They are integrated into the Life Libraries, but they can be purchased individually.

See the back of this book for details on a variety of American Life League projects.

American Life League Public Policy Division

This group of competent staff members assesses the pro-life stance of elected officials, provides public policy papers and research to those who are on the side of life, and works to focus attention on the value of every single human being from fertilization on. We are blessed with competent attorneys and researchers in this division and are prepared to help any legislator or policymaker at the local, state or national level.

Paul and I face the future deeply committed to stopping the killing of innocent babies, through increased education.

We do not accept the "personally opposed" or "I'm pro life, but" arguments from those elected to serve the people. Clearly, if you and I don't expect them to take a clear stand, don't teach others how to effectively oppose such anti-life posturing, and don't demand total protection for all innocent human beings, who will?

∽

ALL and I are committed to seeing the day—in the not-too-distant future—when the killing will end, when the innocent and defenseless will be protected, and when our hard-earned tax dollars are no longer being spent to peddle death and the destruction of the family. We want to see a strong, vigorous, united pro-life movement, with an effective presence in every town, every city, and every state in our nation. We are committed to helping each and every person who is on our side so that one day America will just say no to abortion, and the killing will stop at last. Write to us. We can help you make a difference.

∽

Afterword

Wherever I have come from, I am still going forth. Wherever I have been, I hope I have made a difference. Whatever I have done, it has really been the Lord working through me, since by myself I can do nothing.

Mother Teresa has said that she is nothing but a pencil in the hand of God. Oh, that I might be such an instrument!

I have laid my life before you, not to draw attention to myself, but in the hope that seeing how God has worked through another ordinary person will motivate you to turn to the Lord and ask, "Lord, what would you have me do?"

I began writing this book at my stepfather's house early in 1991. I had traveled to Southern California to be with him because he had suffered another major heart attack, from which he almost died. I returned often to spend a few days with him. My husband, Paul, and our children were so gracious in allowing me the freedom to go. They know how much I cherished Daddy, the man who truly established in my mind the image of the Good Samaritan—ever prepared to do anything he could for his loved ones, his coworkers and those in need. He never complained, you know, even during that last visit to the hospital. His suffering during the last couple of years never got in the way of his loving. He truly appreciated the life God had bestowed on him, and even in his frailty, or perhaps because of it, he spoke only of the positive—rarely of the negative.

When I think of Daddy . . . when I look at the miracles the Lord has done in my own life . . . when I think of what miracles He is able to do in your life as well . . . I know that one day the killing will stop. Our Lord is too merciful, and too powerful, for it to be otherwise.

But He has chosen to do His work through us, the weak things of the earth. Have we yielded ourselves to His power and purpose as fully as we should? Have we pleaded with Him as earnestly as we should for an end to the slaughter? For forgiveness of our country for the grave sin of abortion? For a renewal of our own commitment to His lordship in our lives? Have we thanked Him lately for loving us more than we could ever imagine?

Following is one of my favorite passages from a layman's version of St. Thomas Aquinas. I think it will encourage you, as much as it does me, each and every time I read the words:

A Reflection on God from St. Thomas Aquinas

"We are not hidden from God by our cowering, nor is our reaching for Him a matter of distance. He is indeed not far from any one of us; rather, He is in us, as He is in every created thing, profoundly, intimately, more present to us than we are to ourselves. Our very being, and the being of everything we have, we are, or we meet is a borrowed thing, as the firelight is a loan from the flames. An instant of separation from God would be instant annihilation, for every moment of our life is nourished from the very life of God, more dependent on that life than an infant in the womb is upon the life of the mother. Our hearts can wander far from God, but God is not far from our hearts for we are more His than our own."[1]

GOD LOVES YOU! ASK FOR HIS HELP! WITH HIM AND THROUGH HIM VICTORY IS ASSURED.

[1]Walter Farrell, O.P., S.T.M. and Martin J. Healy, S.T.D., *My Way of Life: Pocket Edition of St. Thomas; The Summa Simplified for Everyone*, Confraternity of the Precious Blood, 1952, p. 12.

RESOURCES

American Life League publishes more than 80 separate resource items that

can be used to combat the evils of abortion, euthanasia, permissive sex instruction, family abuse and more.

Please complete the coupon below to receive a full listing of these valuable resources, along with an order blank for your convenience.

And should you require specific information about any of the work American Life League is doing, please let us know by using the coupon below.

CLIP & MAIL TO:

American Life League

Educational Resources
P.O. Box 1350,
Stafford, VA
22555

Please send the resource catalogue and order blank.
Please send me more information about the following:

_____

PLEASE PRINT:

Name _____

Address_____

City _____

State _____ Zip _____

Phone (_____) _____